Allyn Rickett

I Peter 3:15

HE CLAIMED TO BE GOD

▼

JESUS AND THE ATTRIBUTES OF GOD

Allyn Ricketts, PhD

WESTBOW
PRESS®
A DIVISION OF THOMAS NELSON
& ZONDERVAN

WestBow Press books may be ordered through booksellers or by contacting:

WestBow Press
A Division of Thomas Nelson & Zondervan
1663 Liberty Drive
Bloomington, IN 47403
www.westbowpress.com
844-714-3454

ISBN: 978-1-6642-2492-6 (sc)
ISBN: 978-1-6642-2493-3 (hc)
ISBN: 978-1-6642-2491-9 (e)

Library of Congress Control Number: 2021903610

Print information available on the last page.

WestBow Press rev. date: 03/18/2021

To Rachel for putting up with
me, and always being an
amazing wife, mother, and Nana.

CONTENTS

CONTENTS

ACKNOWLEDGEMENTS

THERE HAVE BEEN many influences on me throughout writing this book. Most of these influences have been cited in the course of the writing. But to others I wish to give an extra note of thanks. I would like to thank Brad Hellein and Jessica Andrews for reading over the manuscript and helping with important corrections, Joshua Ricketts for technical help, as well as Dr. Gary Bailey (Biblical Life Institute/Kairos Project) for the time and support offered to get this project started.

Thanks also goes to the staff at WestBow for their guidance in the process of completing this book and to Pamela Cangioli and her staff for editing help on the manuscript. I would also like to thank all of those who made comments on Facebook over the years denying the deity of Jesus, because they helped keep my enthusiasm up for this project.

Allyn Ricketts, February 2021, Latrobe, PA.

INTRODUCTION

ONE TALK STARTED it all. The idea for this book started about 30 years ago with a conversation following a ministerial association meeting. We were having a discussion in the parking lot outside of a mainline denominational church (not my own denomination) and in that discussion, the pastor of that particular church made the assertion that Jesus never claimed to be God. After I kidded him about the seminary he had gone to, followed by him giving me a hard time about not being up on current theological trends, we moved on to other pastoral concerns. But the notion that Jesus never claimed to be God has been a focus of mine ever since that discussion.

Working in apologetics, I have paid attention to the critical voices of our culture, and also within the church. I continue to hear the frequent claim that Jesus never said he was God. It is common to hear statements like, "We should not hold to the uniqueness of Jesus and we should not hold him in higher esteem than other religious leaders and founders, because he did not claim to be God. Such a claim was invented by the early church."

William Lane Craig points to the central issue when he says:

> Those who deny that Jesus made any personal claims implying divinity face the very severe problem of explaining how it is that the worship of Jesus as Lord and God came about at all in the

early church. It does little good to say that the early church wrote its beliefs about Jesus back into the Gospels, for the problem is the very origin of those beliefs themselves. [Several scholars have shown] that within twenty years of the crucifixion a full-blown Christology proclaiming Jesus as God incarnate existed. How does one explain this worship by monotheistic Jews of one of their countrymen who they had accompanied during his lifetime, apart from the claims of Jesus himself? (Craig 2008, 300).

If Jesus never made the claim to deity, why would the early church have held such a belief from its earliest days? One argument suggests that the claim to deity is merely part of the myth and legend that grew over time. After all, stories and legends about the lives of famous people do tend to grow and evolve as time passes. But that is the problem, isn't it? Legends take time to develop and spread, and yet this belief comes from the earliest records and the earliest manuscripts of the New Testament documents. The proclamation so early of something as dramatic as the divinity of Jesus—so early, in fact, that there were many alive who could have brought evidence to the contrary, if they had some—would have stopped the growth of the myth from the beginning. As G. C. Berkouwer said, "The self-proclamation of Christ has been so unmistakable and clear that it aroused, already during his sojourn on earth, the most vehement opposition. In the gospels, there is not the slightest attempt to transvalue the self-witness of Christ or to rob it of its content, as happened many times in later ages" (Berkouwer 1955, 170).

Berkouwer goes on to point out, as will be discussed later in this book, that those who heard Jesus speak attempted to kill him on more than one occasion because they understood his claim to be God as an assertion both clear and blasphemous. Jesus never equivocated to take the pressure off or to make it more pleasing to the listeners. Jesus made the claim, and the consequences followed him to the cross.

As the following pages review the various ways Jesus claimed to be God, some might notice that this builds a case for the starting point of C. S. Lewis's famous trilemma (Lewis 1971, 56). I think it does even more than make this case, but it does at least establish the foundational point of his argument. Lewis held that if Jesus claimed to be God and he was not, then he was either a madman or a liar. The argument could be set up this way ...

1. Jesus claimed to be God.
2. Jesus either told the truth and he is God, or he lied and is a bad man (or mad).
3. Jesus is not a bad man (or mad).
   Therefore Jesus was (is) God.

It is obvious that, if Jesus claimed to be God and he is not, then he is also not a great religious leader or a great moral teacher. Lying about such a central point would remove him from both of those categories. Some folks attack this notion by saying that Jesus was, in fact, insane. They mean this at least in the sense that he was sincerely wrong. But this still leaves us on the bad side of the equation: Even if Jesus was not morally bad, we end up with a Jesus who is at least no more trustworthy than a liar. Liar or lunatic are not options in Lewis's thinking, because of the very nature of Jesus. Even unbelievers and pagans want to admit that Jesus was good and wise.

Some inside the church deny the historic Christian doctrines and want the faith to be little more than a social movement—yet they would still want to uphold Jesus as good and wise. But, as Peter Kreeft and Ronald Tacelli (Kreeft and Tacelli, 1994, 159) point out, lunatics are not wise, and liars are not good. They point out that, when people think they are God, we expect to see a corresponding sense of ego. There is a self-love and pride. Psychologically, they exhibit an inability to love others as well as a tendency to act irrationally. But all of the things an insane person would do if they thought they were God are the opposite of what we see in the life of Jesus.

Kreeft and Tacelli add that, if Jesus were a liar, the lie was a whopper.

> This would be the biggest and most evil lie in history. It would have caused millions to believe when there is nothing to believe. It would mean centuries of people changing their lives for no reason and trusting their spiritual lives to someone who is dead and gone. Whole cultures basing their moral foundation on the teaching of one who was a liar and a fraud cannot be seen as a good thing. But what we see in Jesus, what all who knew Jesus saw in him, is a morally perfect, unselfish, compassionate, sacrificial person who was also passionate about truth (Kreeft and Tacelli, 1994, 160).

So, could Jesus have been a liar? We see that Jesus simply did not act like a liar. Beyond this, there was no motive for him to lie, since what he taught only brought suffering and death. Maybe most importantly, he took his teaching to his fellow Jews: the ones who were the most unlikely people in the world to believe that God would become a creature. Then could Jesus have been a lunatic? We must say again he did not act like one. He shows no God-complex. A person with such a complex doesn't personally challenge you or inspire you to be more like them. Yet Jesus seemed to have that kind of challenging and inspiring effect on many people. People were attracted to Jesus, not put off by him. It is also true that we might, at times, feel uncomfortable around someone with mental illness because we have abilities or gifts they do not have.

But being around Jesus did just the opposite. Jesus made people uncomfortable because he had gifts and abilities they did not have (Kreeft and Tacelli, 1994, 160-161).

Besides liar, lunatic, or Lord there is fourth option that Lewis did not talk about, but anyone who has gone to seminary in the last seventy-five years has heard about. The idea is that the whole Christian thing is a myth that arose after the time of Jesus and was created by his apostles. But this brings us back to questions similar to the one raised by Craig, above. What is the foundation of this myth? Who was deceived first? Where did the deception come from? Could a lie have the impact this message has had on history? How do you create such a story when people who know the truth are still around? If the early church made these things up, why did they then hold onto them through a century of persecution and martyrdom?

But even this fourth option, when we look closer, turns out not to be the final option proposed in our day. Coming out of the New Age spirituality and the general pluralism of our culture, there is the notion that Jesus was just another guru or avatar. In this position, held by people who often claim to not be religious but consider themselves "spiritual," all the statements of Jesus were spiritual and mystical but certainly not to be taken literally. Jesus knew he was a god just as we all are gods, if we only knew it. He merely was showing us an enlightenment that we all could participate in.

The problem with this, which will be discussed in more detail in chapter 2, is that Jesus was not a Hindu—he was a Jew, and Jewish culture and religion had no concept of eastern mysticism and did not confuse the Creator with the creation. As Kreeft and Tacelli point out, a Jew would not claim to be God. One could be stoned and, as in Jesus's case, crucified for making such a claim. Saying we are all gods was not considered enlightenment, but blasphemy.

In response to these kinds of denials, I am going to combine in this book two areas you might not have put together before.

Most of the chapters will begin with a look at one of the attributes of God, and then look at the words of Jesus that, in one way or another, claim that exact attribute for himself—thus claiming to be God. These attributes of God are our way of organizing the things we see in Scripture concerning the nature of God. The Bible does not organize such attributes, but it is one way Christians have attempted, throughout history, to systematize what the Bible says about who God is and what God is like.

A couple of things are very important to remember. First: We are not saying that these attributes are just our conception of God or just in our mind. The attributes are real aspects of a real God with real being. What we see revealed in Scripture concerning the nature of God is real. Because God is infinite, and we are finite, our understanding of the nature of God does not come to us as a single idea or notion. The Scripture describes various aspects of God's nature, and then we naturally bring our own needs, interests, and presuppositions to the Scriptures. All of this leads us to focus on one attribute over another and give them definition. Beyond this, we must remember that, while our finite mind might grasp only a partial view of the full nature of God, our limitations do not limit the nature or being of God. We might organize this information to help us understand and remember, but we are not saying that the attributes of God are just our conceptualization. As Charles Hodge pointed out, we must understand and admit that, "the divine perfections are really what the Bible declares them to be; that God truly thinks, feels, and acts; that He is truly wise, just, and good; that He is truly omnipotent, and voluntary, acting or not acting, as He sees fit; that He can hear and answer prayer" (Hodge 1997, 1:373-374).

In addition, when we talk about God's attributes, we are not talking simply about what God does or the way God acts. We are talking about God's nature. For instance, some might say that we call God just only because we see that God acts justly. Yet this notion seems contrary to what we see in Scripture, where justice is the very nature of God, the very foundation of his throne (Psalm 89:14). The acts of God are just because it is God's nature to be just.

It is also important to remember that when Christians speak of the attributes of God, we do not mean that these attributes are different building blocks of God, as if you could add them all together and get God. It is not that one part of God is holy and another part loving, and still another part just. That is, when we say God is holy, we do not see holiness as a part of God, but rather that all that God is, is holy. When we speak of God's justice, we do not mean that one aspect of God expresses his justice, but rather that all of God's thoughts, actions, and God's very being, are just.

The God of the Bible is a unity and diversity. There is great comfort in knowing that God is unchanging and even more comfort in knowing that he cares for each of us individually and personally. So God might be unchanging in his nature and yet, because of his personal care for each person, also respond on the basis of that nature differently to each of our diverse circumstances. This is why it is so misleading and limiting to make a statement like, "Well, my God is a God of love." Because all of God's attributes function in complete harmony, theologians often speak of the *simplicity* of God. But, as we will see, God is also infinite and unbounded in his being. So we need to understand that while our finite minds might grasp only a partial view of the full nature of God, to think of only one of God's attributes as the defining aspect of God is like picking one color on a multicolored beach ball and saying "I like to think of this ball as red." You are, in fact, thinking of a different ball if the one you are thinking of is only red—and you are thinking of a different God if the one you are thinking of is only love. We need to remember that these attributes are part of God's very nature. They do not come and go, and they do not fade away. They are the very nature of God, and God's nature cannot be distinguished from his essence. They are what we mean, and what we are describing, when we use the word *God*.

Even though these attributes of God have been organized in a number of different ways by theologians, one of the most common is to designate them as Incommunicable and Communicable. The Incommunicable attributes are the ones only God possesses. There is nothing in humans, or any part of creation, which is similar or analogous to these attributes. Omnipotence, for example, is incommunicable. No part of the creation, or even the creation as a whole, can be said to be omnipotent.

The communicable attributes are those which God has shared in a limited way with those created in God's image. Here we find in humans some attributes that are similar to certain attributes of God. The attribute is not the same, but there is an analogy or likeness. For instance, God is love and acts lovingly. He has shared that attribute, in a finite way, with his human creatures, so that we may also give and receive love.

Jesus claimed these divine attributes, especially the incommunicable, for himself. Did Jesus ever actually claim to be God? Yes, and he did so on nearly every page of the Gospels. He did so by claiming and displaying the attributes of God, primarily the incommunicable ones.

This book seeks to pull together in one place the ways in which Jesus claimed to be God. None of this is exactly new. The ideas can be found in many theology books and books on the text of the New Testament. But my hope is that having them in one place will help us to see the power and the clarity of the claims of Christ.

The claim that Jesus is God raises an issue we need to look at right at the beginning of our discussion. I stood on my front porch one day, as I have many times, talking to a Jehovah's Witness. When I claimed that Jesus was God. He asked, "Then who was Jesus praying to when he prayed?" The answer to this question involves the doctrine of the Trinity. The Trinity always seems to come into the discussion when you talk about Jesus being God. If Jesus is God, and God the Father is God, then the Trinity naturally presents itself.

The next chapter will look at the doctrine of the Trinity, to lay a foundation for examining the claims of Jesus.

CHAPTER ONE

▼

THE TRINITY

AS WE BEGIN to look at the attributes Jesus claimed to possess, we ought to note that the notion of Jesus being God raises some questions that direct us to the doctrine of the Trinity. If Jesus is God, and God is God, yet we believe in only one God, then we are going to have to think in terms of something like the Trinity. Why should we believe in such a doctrine? The idea is difficult to get our minds around and it certainly is unique to the Christian faith. It is a doctrine that depends entirely on the revelation God has given us in the Bible. We would not have arrived at this concept by just thinking about God or even looking at the creation and building a natural theology.

When a critic asks, "If Jesus is God, who was he praying to?" I point out to the critic or the cult member that this is not a problem for the Christian: Christians believe in the Trinity, so it's possible for us to understand that Jesus was talking to the Father. This is not a problem for Christians who recognize the perfect communication, fellowship, and agreement between the Father, Son, and Holy Spirit.

The doctrine of the Trinity—or the triunity of God—is the

means by which Christians explain what is taught in Scripture about the nature of God, Jesus, and the Holy Spirit. Some critics argue that the word *trinity* is not in the Bible. My response is, so what? Many of the words we use in theology and biblical studies are not in the Bible. There is no reason not to use an appropriate word to describe a doctrine, even if that word doesn't appear in the Bible. The question is whether the doctrine itself is found in, or is based upon, Scripture. Scripture is our final authority.

Looking back in history we see that the early believers were faced with a three-pronged dilemma. First, both the Old Testament and the New Testament clearly taught that there is only one God. Early Christians and Jews agreed on this, and we still do. Monotheism was the core commitment of the early believers' faith. But then comes the second part of the problem. There are teachings in the New Testament that Jesus is God. This book will present a part of the argument for this as we look at the ways Jesus made this claim about himself. It is, though, only a part of the evidence. The third part of the problem is that the New Testament documents also make it plain that the Holy Spirit is God—not just the force or power of God but that the Holy Spirit is a personality. This claim about the Holy Spirit is not the focus of this book, but we need to look briefly at the scriptural support for it, because the idea of the Trinity is inextricably connected to the understanding that Jesus is God, and the deity and personality of the Holy Spirit is directly connected to understanding the Trinity.

In Matthew 12:31–32, we see our first glimpse of the nature of the Holy Spirit. In this passage Jesus had just healed a demon-possessed man, and this healing brought him into a debate with the Pharisees. It is at this point that Jesus explains about blasphemy against the Holy Spirit: "Therefore I say to you, any sin and blasphemy shall be forgiven people, but blasphemy against the Spirit shall not be forgiven. Whoever speaks a word against the Son of Man, it shall be forgiven him; but whoever speaks against the Holy Spirit, it shall not be forgiven him, either in this age or in the age to come."

Jesus spoke here of blasphemy against the Holy Spirit—but one can only blaspheme God. Jesus was assigning deity status to the Holy Spirit. To blaspheme against Jesus is one thing, and serious enough, but to blaspheme the Holy Spirit is a whole other kind of error. Such blasphemy requires an intentional rejection of the work of the Spirit—the very work that leads to repentance and the finding of salvation.

Then, in Matthew 28:19, Jesus was giving some final teaching to the disciples, including the Great Commission to go into all the world to make disciples. As disciples are made, baptism would follow, and we see here the baptism formula as given by Jesus, "Go therefore and make disciples of all the nations, baptizing them in the name of the Father and the Son and the Holy Spirit." In saying this, Jesus put the Holy Spirit on the same level and in the same context as the Father and the Son. There is no hint of inequality.

Moving on to the book of Acts, Luke brings us to the remarkable events around Ananias and Sapphira. In Acts 5:3-4, Luke describes Peter responding to the bad example set by the actions of Ananias and Sapphira. At the end of chapter 4, Barnabas was presented as a good example when he sold a tract of land and gave the money to the apostles. Ananias and Sapphira appeared to do the same thing, but they held back a portion. It is true that they had every right to hold back some of what was theirs—but they pretended to have given it all to God, when they had not. They put on a false front to look good. Peter pointed out that they had lied to the Holy Spirit, and to lie to the Holy Spirit is to lie to God.

"But Peter said, 'Ananias, why has Satan filled your heart to lie to the Holy Spirit and to keep back some of the price of the land? While it remained unsold, did it not remain your own? And after it was sold, was it not under your control? Why is it that you have conceived this deed in your heart? You have not lied to men but to God.'" Peter therefore affirms by his response that the Holy Spirit is God, since to lie to one is to lie to the other.

In 1 Corinthians 2:10-11, Paul adds to what Peter has said and tells us more about the Holy Spirit. "For to us God revealed them through the Spirit; for the Spirit searches all things, even the depths of God. For who among men knows the thoughts of a man except the spirit of the man which is in him? Even so the thoughts of God no one knows except the Spirit of God." It is not that the Spirit is looking for more knowledge but that the Spirit already possesses the knowledge of God—the knowledge and thoughts of God are the knowledge and thoughts of the Holy Spirit. This gives the Holy Spirit the attribute of omniscience, an attribute only applicable to God (and an attribute, as we will see, also claimed by Jesus).

This Holy Spirit is the same Spirit who spoke to Moses. Paul tells us this in 2 Corinthians 3:12-18, where he reminds us that, as a result of the presence of the Holy Spirit, Moses had to veil his face. Paul used this image to suggest that there is still a veil between God and humanity until we turn to God. He makes it clear in verse 17 that "now the Lord is the Spirit." And then in verse 18 he says, "But we all, with unveiled face, beholding as in a mirror the glory of the Lord, are being transformed into the same image from glory to glory, just as from the Lord, the Spirit." Paul speaks of the Lord and the Spirit as the same, one God.

Paul does not stop with the Father and the Holy Spirt but adds the Son in Ephesians 4:4–6, where he once again speaks of all three persons of the Trinity in the same breath and on the same level. All three are there, but there is only one God, and the Spirit is fully a part of that triunity. "There is one body and one Spirit, just as also you were called in one hope of your calling; one Lord, one faith, one baptism, one God and Father of all who is over all and through all and in all." We might add to this that, just as Jesus put all three persons of the Trinity on the same level, so did Paul in 2 Corinthians 13:14, where he gave a Trinitarian benediction: "The grace of the Lord Jesus Christ, and the love of God, and the fellowship of the Holy Spirit, be with you all." Paul saw the Holy Spirit as coequal with the Father and the Son.

All of these Scriptures clearly teach us that the Holy Spirit is God, but taken alone, these verses could still just refer to the power of God and not a distinct personage within the Godhead. But we can find in Scripture a number of references that show us the personality of the Holy Spirit. We will look at a few of them briefly to make our case.

In Luke 12:10-12 we see Jesus's teaching about the blasphemy against the Holy Spirit, as noted above. However, as we look more closely we also see that Jesus claimed that the Holy Spirit would teach them what they needed to say at the right moment when they would be making their defense of the faith. Only a person teaches, and the Holy Spirit does so. In John 14:26, in Jesus's most detailed description of the Holy Spirit, he told the apostles that the Holy Spirit would not just teach but would help them remember what they needed to know. This was, in some sense, Jesus commissioning the New Testament as the promise of the inspiration of the Spirit was given to the apostles. But it also tells us more of the personal actions of the Holy Spirit. In this section of John 14-16, Jesus tells us even more. In 15:26, Jesus refers to the Holy Spirit as a *helper* and as one who will bear witness. In these passages, Jesus consistently referred to the Holy Spirit as a *Him* or *He*.

Some might see these passages as anthropomorphisms. It is true, we can learn from inanimate objects; we might even say that they can guide us in a specific direction. It should not be missed, however, that some of these passages must mean personality. John 16:8 tells us that the Holy Spirit will convict the world of its sin. This kind of conviction would certainly seem to require a personal touch, as well as the passing on of information concerning the judgment. There is even more to this. Just a few verses later, in verse 13, Jesus said that the Holy Spirit will guide, speak, hear, and disclose what is to come. These are certainly the actions of a personal being. But this is not all—because Jesus went on to say that the Holy Spirit will glorify him as the Spirit discloses more and more about him. Again, this is the action of a personal being and another hint of the inspiration of the New Testament.

So, the Holy Spirit can speak, and this is not an isolated claim. In Acts 8:29; 11:12; and 13:2 we also see that the Holy Spirit speaks. Then in Acts 15:28 we are told that, "For it seemed good to the Holy Spirit and to us to lay upon you no greater burden than these essentials." Here, it seems the Holy Spirit is capable of rational thought, of reasoning something out. This not the description of merely the power of God. Could something impersonal forbid us to do something? That is exactly what Acts 16:6-7 tells us the Holy Spirit did when Paul and his companions wanted to speak the word in Asia. These verses tell us they were forbidden by the Holy Spirit to do so. In the same sentence, the Holy Spirit is referred to as the "Spirit of Jesus" when the Spirit prevented them from entering Bithynia. If Jesus is personal and this is his Spirit—and if the Spirit can act clearly enough to forbid something—then the Spirit is more than just the power of God.

Paul understood this when he claimed in Romans 8:16 that, "The Spirit Himself bears witness with our spirit that we are children of God." The act of bearing witness is a personal act, similar to the work of the Spirit in Galatians 4:6 where we are told, "And because you are sons, God has sent forth the Spirit of His Son into our hearts, crying, 'Abba! Father'!" The Spirit bears witness with our spirit as he enters our hearts and speaks, and cries out in worship. Since the Spirit indwells us in this personal manner, it is therefore possible for our lives to bring grief to the Spirit. Inanimate forces do not grieve— yet Ephesians 4:30 tells us the Spirit can be grieved by us. It is also this kind of personal communication that Peter spoke of in 1 Peter 1:11 when he talked about the "Spirit of Christ" speaking to the prophets. So we have in Scripture the Holy Spirit spoken of as God and as personal. We have Jesus spoken of as God with us in the fullness of deity. We also have one personal God, spoken of as Father.

In addition to all we have mentioned, Scripture shows us the three persons interacting. The Son prayed to the Father (John 17). The Father spoke from heaven about the Son (Matthew 3:15-17), and the Holy Spirit made an appearance at the same time. There are also descriptions of their differing roles in salvation: the Father planned it (John 3:16; Ephesians 1:4), the Son accomplished it on the cross (John 17:4; 19:30), and in the resurrection (Romans 4:25; 1 Corinthians 15:1-6), but the Holy Spirit applies it to the lives of believers (John 3:5; Ephesians 4:30; Titus 3:5-7).

The early believers were faced with the question of what to do with all of this information? How were they to put these complex ideas together in any logical way? There was some struggle in the early church as to just how to speak of these ideas and how to formulate them accurately so that none of the three persons of the Trinity was slighted or misrepresented. This was a serious struggle, and yet the debate and struggle itself shows that the knowledge behind the formulation of the doctrine of the Trinity was there from the very beginning. Hints of the Trinity can even be found in the Old Testament. Clearly, the idea of the Trinity was not fully revealed until the New Testament, but we might suspect that if this is truly the nature of God, there might be hints of it even in the Old Testament. Many claim this to, in fact, be the case. One place pointed to is the very first few verses of the Bible, Genesis 1:1-3, give us some clues (Erickson 1995, 328-329): "In the beginning God created the heavens and the earth. The earth was formless and void, and darkness was over the surface of the deep, and the Spirit of God was moving over the surface of the waters. Then God said, 'Let there be light'; and there was light." We learn in the New Testament that Jesus is the Word of God. So here we have God Creating, the Spirit moving over the creation, and the Word bringing the light as God spoke the creation into being.

Some see another hint found early in Genesis. Genesis 1:26, says, "Then God said, 'Let Us make man in Our image, according to Our likeness; and let them rule over the fish of the sea and over the birds of the sky and over the cattle and over all the earth, and over every creeping thing that creeps on the earth.'" It is important to note that this is not the only place in the Old Testament where God uses this *Us* language. We can also see it in Genesis 3:22 and 11:7 as well as in Isaiah 6:8 at the point of Isaiah's call to be a prophet. It is suggested that this language is possibly similar to the *royal we* and just designates God's sovereign position. The problem is that we do not find the royal we or plural of intensity used in language for more than a thousand years after Moses. The royal we was never used by a king in Israel. It was not part of the language (Archer 1982, 359).

Others say that when God says *Us*, he is just addressing himself, since there was no one else to speak to. But does an infinite God really have this problem? Could not such a God use the singular if, in fact, that God is not a trinity? The God of the Bible does sometimes speak in the singular, using *I* and *My* when speaking to his people. Thus we see the plurality when he is speaking to himself and the unity when he communicates with his creatures.

Another common suggestion is that God is speaking to the angels. While the first two suggestions might work in a grammatical sense, the third makes no sense at all, since human beings were not created in the image of angels—and we ought to add that the angels are not God's counselors. Instead, God's words leave us with a hint of the persons of the Trinity in relationship with each other at the foundation of creation and on into Biblical history.

While looking at Genesis, some attention should be given to Genesis 2:24. This is a verse I have always used to describe the biblical definition of marriage when helping couples prepare for their wedding. It reads, "For this reason a man shall leave his father and his mother, and be joined to his wife; and they shall become one flesh." What is important for our discussion is the word "one," which here obviously means one consisting of two. This word, *echod* in Hebrew, is also used in the events of Numbers 13, where Moses sent spies out to check the land of Canaan. The spies cut a huge cluster of grapes and brought it back on a pole carried between them. Verse 23 tells us, "Then they came to the valley of Eshcol and from there cut down a branch with a single cluster of grapes;

and they carried it on a pole between two men, with some of the pomegranates and the figs." In the words "single cluster" we see in Hebrew again the word *echod*, telling us that we have one thing made up of many; a diversity in the context of a unity.

There is another very powerful use of the word *echod* which adds evidence to the claim that the word speaks of a unity in a diversity. The Shema—the central verse of Judaism found in Deuteronomy 6:4—clearly describes the Jewish focus on monotheism by speaking of God being "One": "Hear, O Israel! The LORD is our God, the LORD is one!" This verse clearly intends to tell us that God is *one* being and one essence. Yet this very verse, found on the door posts of many Jewish homes, uses the word *echod* to make the point. Is this a hint of the Trinity at the center of Old Testament teaching?

When we add these ideas to the statements in Genesis 19:24 and Isaiah 44:6 that speak of more than one Yahweh, we see clear indications of the Trinity—unless we are going to accept polytheism. For example Isaiah 44:6 tells us

> Thus says the LORD [Yahweh], the King of Israel
> And his Redeemer, the LORD [Yahweh] of hosts

Is there more than one Yahweh or is the Trinity in view here? Then there is the interesting wording of Isaiah 48:16. In this passage, Yahweh is identified as the speaker. This identification happens particularly in verse 12, where the speaker says, "I am the first, I am the last," which identifies the speaker with Yahweh of 44:6. So the one speaking is Yahweh when he says, "Come near to Me, listen to this: From the first I have not spoken in secret, From the time it took place, I was there. And now the Lord GOD has sent Me, and His Spirit." Here we have Yahweh speaking of being sent by Yahweh along with Yahweh's Spirit. Given all of this, the evidence comes together pretty strongly to support the notion that we can find the Trinity in the Old Testament.

What We Do Not Mean By 'Trinity'

Since the thesis of this book is that Jesus was claiming to be God, and therefore one person of the Trinity, it is important that we understand what Christians have and have not meant by the Trinity. First, we must say that we do not mean three different gods. We do not believe in tritheism. There are not three gods, but rather only one God. This is often misunderstood, even after two thousand years of Christian monotheism, more often than I would like to think. Sometimes there seems to be an intentional misrepresentation by skeptics, and sometimes it seems to be a misunderstanding on the part of the hearer. For instance, Muslims believe that Christians have three gods. Muhammad said, "O Jesus, son of Mary! Didst thou say unto mankind: Take me and my mother for two gods beside Allah?" (Surah 5:116) Muhammad seemed to think the Trinity was God, Jesus, and Mary. But the Trinity has never meant that.

Second, it is important to realize that Christians do not mean that God merely worked through Jesus. We mean more by the Trinity than that God was just a dominant force in Jesus (or on Jesus). Throughout Christian history there have been those who have held that Jesus was just a human in whom God (or the "God Force") worked in a special way. This view has been called Dynamic Monarchianism. The *dynamis* or power of God ruled (hence the term *monarch*) over the human Jesus, who was just an ordinary man until, at his baptism, the power of God or the Christ Spirit descended upon him and enabled him to perform the miracles he accomplished. This is one form of adoptionism, where Jesus becomes the chosen one at some point during his life. This view has a parallel in New Age thought today, where it is said that we might all have the Christ Spirit if we could be as enlightened as Jesus. This view is a denial of the Trinity, because in this view, Jesus does not share in the substance of the Father. This view would also deny the deity of Jesus and so is not what historic Christianity has taught.

Third, we need to see that historic Christianity does not teach that there are merely three aspects or modes of one God. This view, called Modalism, gained some support in the third century. Modalism taught that there is one God who may be referred to as Father, Son, or Holy Spirit. In this way of thinking, the names do not represent real distinctions within God, but are really only names that are appropriate at different times. It may be said under this view that God revealed himself as Father, and then later in time, as the Son, and even later, as the Holy Spirit—but all of this was just God communicating in three different ways. A leader in this movement was Sabellius, and so the idea of Modalism is often referred to as Sabellianism.

Some groups today, usually referred to as *Oneness Churches*, still hold this view, but it is not the teaching of the Christian faith. We mean much more than this when we speak of the Trinity. At least Modalism was an attempt at something like the Trinity or an explanation of the problem of what to do with a divine God, a divine Son, and a divine Holy Spirit. Their answer was to teach that there was not one essential God existing in three persons, but rather just one God with three different names, roles, or actions.

The Christian Church rejected this idea entirely, and did so partly because of what Modalism cannot answer. Modalism cannot explain those places in Scripture which speak of the persons of the Trinity working and functioning and in communication with one another, all at the same time. Sometimes the persons of the Trinity appear simultaneously, such as at Jesus's baptism. Modalism also did just the opposite of Monarchianism in that it denied the true humanity of Jesus and saw Jesus as just a mode or extension of God. In this view, Jesus only appeared to be human (Docetism). If Modalism is true, then Jesus was misleading those around him by allowing a distinct voice, as if from the Father, to speak at his baptism. Christians do need to be careful at this point, because many of the illustrations used to describe the Trinity—such as water being liquid, a solid, and a gas—actually lead to a Modalistic view of the Trinity.

A fourth idea that we are not affirming when we speak about the Trinity is the idea that Jesus and/or the Holy Spirit are lesser gods than God the Father. This again was the teaching of a third century group call the Arians, named after their founder, Arius. Arians held that Jesus was sort of a lower-class god who was higher than the angels but less than Yahweh God. Jesus was seen as the first created being. This view carries on today as the specific teaching of the Jehovah's Witnesses. The historic Christian claim is that the Son and Holy Spirit are equal to, and one in substance with, the Father.

What We Do Mean By 'Trinity'

In response to the teachings of Arius and Sabellius, the church had to finally make explicit what it had believed since the beginning. It also had to find a way to explain it clearly. This took shape in a strong way at the Council of Nicaea in A.D. 325. The most famous person in the debates that took place there was probably Athanasius (who lived from 293 to 373) as he responded to Arius. Athanasius led the way in formulating the doctrine, and others helped refine it at the Council of Constantinople in 381. These councils did not invent the doctrine or even the name *Trinity*, which had been used by Tertullian a full century before the Council of Nicaea. The important statement at Nicaea was that God was one *ousia* or substance and three *hypostasis* or persons. That is it held God to be one substance and three substructures, referring to the persons of the Father, Son, and Holy Spirit. These persons are not merely alongside each other, but in a sense, permeate one another—and yet, each is a person.

Personal pronouns such as *I, He,* and *Him* are used of each of the three persons and for God in general. Just as some object to the use of the word *Trinity,* others object to the use of the word *person* for the members of the Trinity, since the word is not used in Scripture.

"But if there be but one God, and the Son be Divine, the distinction cannot be one of essence, and must, therefore, be a *personal* one. This seems sufficient to use the word 'person' in discussing the doctrine of the Trinity" (Field 1952, 112).

Christian teaching on the Trinity is our attempt to pull all of these truths together. When we say *Trinity,* we are affirming the unity of God. (The order of topics within this section follows the order from Erickson 1995, 337-338.) The basis of the Trinity is monotheism. Building on this, we affirm the deity of the Father, the Son, and the Holy Spirit. All three are qualitatively the same. All three persons possess all of the divine attributes, yet in the substance of their being, they are one. We are speaking here of a unity, not a singularity.

Then we must affirm—and this is central—that the *oneness* of God and the *threeness* of God are not speaking of the same relationship. The law of contradiction says that A cannot be non-A at the same time and in the same relationship. The claim here is that we are not saying that God is one in substance and three in substance, nor are we saying that God is one person and three persons at the same time. We are saying that God is one in substance and three in person. This constitutes a different relationship and raises no logical error or contradiction. Modalism tried to avoid the appearance of contradiction by placing the three persons at different places in time. Historic Christianity asserts that the difference is in relationship, and so God is three persons at the same time and in all times. Trinity means that God is one and three at the same time, but not in the same relationship or sense. God is one *what* and three *whos,* meaning a unity in essence and plurality in persons.

I have had conversations, particularly with Jehovah's Witnesses in a number of settings, where the claim was made, "But 1+1+1 does *not* equal 1." We can all certainly agree with that math, but we are not adding three persons to get one person. We are saying that there is one substance with three persons, so that all three persons are fully that one substance.

Another aspect of the Trinity that we want to affirm is that the Trinity is eternal. It is important for us to see that we are talking about the very nature of God. God has always been one and three. There always has been Father, Son, and Holy Spirit; the nature of God has never changed. This is important because it brings us to the practical implications of a doctrine that many people think to be quite abstract. One implication is that there always was love. In fact, the notion that God is love requires a Trinity. There must be someone to love.

> All sorts of people are fond of repeating the Christian statement that 'God is love.' But they seem not to notice that the words 'God is love' have no real meaning unless God has at least two Persons. Love is something that one person has for another person. If God was a single person, then before the world was made, He was not love (Lewis 1971, 151).

This is the failure of Unitarianism and the problem for any faith that wants to hold to a monotheism without a Trinity. It is powerful to understand that God was not lonely before the creation. God is entirely self-sufficient and needs no one. Love exists within his nature. This cannot be true without a Trinitarian view. Jonathan Edwards spoke to this same issue in another context in *The Nature of True Virtue*. He claimed that true virtue itself finds its ultimate place in the Trinity.

> From hence also it is evident that the divine virtue, or the virtue of the divine mind, must consist primarily in love to himself, or in the mutual love and friendship which subsists eternally and necessarily between the several persons in the Godhead, or that infinitely strong propensity there

is in these divine persons one to another (Edwards
1957, 8:557).

Then, in the introduction to *A History of the Work of Redemption*,
Edwards claimed that the history he was about to share ultimately
had been carried out by God to glorify the Trinity.

> In all this God designed to accomplish the glory of
> the blessed Trinity in an eminent degree. God had
> a design of glorifying himself from eternity; yea,
> to glorify each person in the Godhead ... It was
> his design that the Son should thus be glorified,
> and should glorify the Father by what should be
> accomplished by the Spirit to the glory of the Spirit,
> that the whole Trinity, conjunctly, and each person
> singly, might be exceedingly glorified (Edwards
> 1974, 1:536).

So the persons of the Trinity are co-equal and are one God. For
example, in speaking of the nature of Christ, Edwards said that,
"there meet in the person of Christ the deepest reverence towards
and equality with God ... God the Father hath no attribute or
perfection that the Son hath not, in equal degree, and equal glory"
(Edwards 1974, 1:682).

In explaining the Christian view of God, Edwards made it
clear that there is no true idea of God unless one is thinking of the
Trinitarian God of the Bible. As we see in the quotations above,
Edwards proclaimed the Christian view that there is no excellence
without plurality. Early in Edwards's writing, he claimed that there
must be some sort of communication or relationship if there is to
be perfection. His claim was that there is no true understanding
of God unless the God being considered is personal, and there is
no true personality in a monism where love and communication
cannot exist.

One alone, without any reference to any more,
cannot be excellent; for in such a case there can
be no manner of relation, and therefore no such
thing as consent. Indeed, what we call "one" may
be excellent, because of a consent of parts, or some
consent of those in that being that are distinguished
into a plurality some way or other. But in a being
that is absolutely without any plurality there cannot
be excellency, for there can be no such thing as
consent or agreement (Edwards 1957, 6:337).

Now Edwards, one of the greatest minds America ever
produced, may be getting a little too philosophical here—but hang
in there for one more quotation, as Edwards expressed that God's
love is indeed based in the nature and the reality of the Trinity.

As to God's excellence, it is evident it consists in
the love of himself. For he was as excellent before
he created the universe as he is now. But if the
excellence of spirits consists in their disposition
and action God could be excellent in no other
way at that time, for all the exertions of himself
were towards himself. But he exerts himself
towards himself no other way than in infinitely
loving and delighting in himself, in the mutual
love of the Father and Son. This makes the third,
the personal Holy Spirit or the holiness of God,
which is his infinite beauty, and this is God's
infinite consent to being in general (Edwards
1957, 6:364).

If, then, God is complete within God's own Trinitarian nature,
then all of this means that God did not *need* to create anything, but
chose to do so.

A leader at a youth retreat I attended used the poem by James Weldon Johnson that speaks of God being lonely and therefore he created man. It is a powerful poem—but if God was alone before the creation, then how was God love? The Trinity tells us that God was not alone, because there always has been Father, Son, and Holy Spirit within God's being.

Because God did not need to create, to be part of the creation is to be part of the desire of God. You are who you are because God wanted you to be you. You are fallen and need redemption, and your fallen feelings may lead you away from who you really are, but you have worth as an image-bearer of God. This understanding of the Trinity also means there always was communication among the persons of the Trinity, and so we see God as a communicating being and we have a foundation for the claim that revelation has taken place in our history. Without a Trinity, it is hard to maintain God's self-sufficiency, because God would have to create in order to have a subject-object relationship. If God is alone and does not exist in the form of a Trinity, then God would have no one to know, love, or communicate with. A personal God would be dependent on the creation, in a Unitarian system.

> The knowledge of God the Father who is the source of redemption, of God the Son who achieves redemption, and of God the Holy Spirit who applies redemption, is declared in Scripture to be eternal life. Every other conception of God presents a false God to the mind and conscience. So different is the system of theology developed, and the manner of life which flows from it, that for all practical purposes we may say that Unitarianism and Trinitarianism worship different Gods" (Boettner 1960, 133).

Boettner goes on to show the importance of this doctrine for the Christian faith. "If there were no Trinity, there could be no incarnation, no objective redemption, and therefore no salvation; for there would then be no one capable of acting as Mediator between God and man" (Boettner 1960, 135).

When Christians use the word *Trinity*, we also are affirming that the function or role of one member of the Trinity might, for a time, be subordinate or under the headship of another member of the Trinity. By this, we do not mean a subordination of essence, but a temporary role. For the specific purpose of salvation by incarnation, Jesus listened to and obeyed the Father. Having allowed himself to become part of the creation, Jesus said his very existence—his food (to use his words from John 4:34)—was to do the will of the Father. He faced this in the Garden of Gethsemane and obeyed. "Yet not My will, but Thine be done" (Luke 22:42).

We also see the Holy Spirit submitting to the ministry of the Son as Jesus tells us in John 14-16. So Scripture tells us that the Father sends the Son (John 17:8; Romans 8:3: 1 Thessalonians 5:9), and the Father and the Son work through the Holy Spirit (Romans 5:5; Galatians 5:22-23; Titus 3:5; Acts 15:8-9) and Jesus says that he sends the Holy Spirit (John 14-16). There is also the interesting passage in 1 Corinthians 11:3 where Paul talks about "God being the head of Christ."

We must finally admit that the Trinity is a mystery. That is not a cop-out. We have been giving reasons to believe in the Trinity for a number of pages now. But what we are saying is that we would never have come to this doctrine on our own; it depends on the special revelation of God found in the Scripture. It is this foundation, based in Scripture, which sets the stage for our understanding of the claims Jesus made for himself.

CHAPTER TWO

▼

THE CLAIM TO BE YAHWEH

FOR MANY YEARS during worship, I would sit down with the children in the front of the sanctuary and share a mini-sermon with the energetic little group. Over the years, I was told several times that the adults also learned much during these messages, which is both good news and a little frightening. However, even I often learned things from the children. Sometimes their insight or the relevance of one of their questions would strike me, and sometimes they just said things out loud about their family that had their parents hiding behind the pews. One question that came up on a couple of occasions over the years was, "Who made God?"

Now, I understand that question coming from a six-year-old, but when it comes from anyone older than that, I get concerned. Either we have completely failed to communicate what we mean by the word *God,* or people are willfully ignoring the Christian claims about the nature of God to suit their own purposes. Maybe it is a little of both.

The Independence of God

The first attribute of God we will look at, relating to Jesus's claim to be God, is what is referred to as the *independence* of God. Some use the word *aseity* to refer to this attribute. *Aseity* brings from its origins the understanding of being self-created or self-originated, which can confuse the issue, since it sounds like God created himself. The word *independence* avoids the idea of a beginning in God and expresses the idea that God is not dependent or contingent upon anything or anyone for his existence.

What Christians are getting at, in discussing this aspect of the nature of God, is that God has, as an attribute, the power *to be*. It is part of God's very nature. God exists by necessity simply because of who God is. It is also important to see that, following from this attribute, God also is independent in all actions, decrees, acts of his will, and so on. This is one of the attributes of God that is not shared with his creation.

That which is created cannot be independent. All of creation is contingent by the very nature of being created, but God is self-existent. God has the power to be. God is independent of all creatures, not only for existence, but for his entire nature. God does not need anyone's help to come into existence or to remain in existence. This aspect of God's independence is taught from the very first verse of the Bible: "In the beginning ... God." All things come from, and are dependent upon, God for their existence.

In Isaiah 40:25–26, God asks:

> "To whom then will you liken Me
> That I should be his equal?" says the Holy One.
> Lift up your eyes on high
> And see who has created these stars
> The One who leads forth their host by number,
> He calls them all by name;

Because of the greatness of His might and the
strength of His power
Not one of them is missing.

Paul, when speaking to the Athenians in Acts 17, spoke of God
as being the Creator of all things in heaven and earth. And as
Creator God, he cannot be bound by the creation, nor by any being,
since he gave to all living beings breath and life. Paul sums all of
this up in Romans 11:36: "For from Him and through Him and to
Him are all things. To Him be glory forever. Amen."

This takes us back to the third chapter of Exodus. Once we have
grasped the independence of God—that the nature of God is to be, to
exist—and when we see that God has the power *to be* as a part of his
nature, then we understand why he chose to be known by the name "I
AM." Remember Moses on Mt. Horeb as he stood before the burning
bush? Moses received the call to return to Pharaoh, but he wasn't sure
if he could handle the assignment. Moses wondered what he would
say if they were to ask who had sent him. What name should he give?
God responds saying that Moses should tell them "I AM" has sent you.

God's very name, the word most sacred in all of Judaism is the
four-letter Hebrew tetragrammaton (YHWH), the name too holy
to be pronounced by Jews. The tetragrammaton, which means "I
AM," gives witness that the power of God to exist is part of God's
nature. Notice also that when God said "I AM," God was *saying*
"I AM." God's being also includes that he is living, personal, and
verbal. God does not derive life from any other source, any more
than God derives being from any other source. God's life is the
source of life; it needs no sustenance.

I grew up in Western Pennsylvania in the era when the Ligonier
Valley Study Center began in Stahlstown. I attended a number of
events there and, for a time, lived close enough to occasionally be
part of a weekly Bible study that Dr. Sproul held for local folks. In
addition to these live events, I have listened to many hours of Dr.
Sproul's teachings, going all the way back to when the lectures

were on cassette tapes. I heard R.C. ask, on many occasions, "If there ever was a time when there was nothing, what would there be now?" I have asked that same question many times myself and I've been amazed that youth often get the answer faster than adults.

If ever there was a time when there was nothing, there would now be nothing. Every student in my Introduction to Philosophy classes comes to know the phrase *ex nihilo nihil fit*. Out of nothing comes nothing. These days, many try to get around this so they can avoid accepting a Creator, but they always seem to slip something into their nothing. Dr. Sproul's point was that, if there is something now, then something must have the power to be. This is what we mean by God being a *necessary being*.

> Does not Christianity assert a universe coming
> from nothing? Do we not assert *ex nihilo* creation?
> Indeed we do. But that "nothing" has reference to
> the absence of a *material cause.* There is a *sufficient
> cause* for the universe. There is an *efficient* cause
> for the universe. There is a God who has within
> Himself to power to create. God has the power
> of being within Himself. Such an assertion is not
> gratuitous nor is it the mere dogmatic assertion
> of religion. It is a dictate of science and reason. If
> something *is,* then something intrinsically has the
> power of being. Somewhere, somehow, something
> must have the *power of being.* If not, we are left with
> only two options: (1) being comes from nothing or
> (2) we are faced with the contradiction, "nothing
> is." Those options would be more miraculous than
> miracle if such were possible (Sproul 1988, 56).

Whenever this argument is made, concerning the need for a Creator, someone usually suggests that maybe the creation has always existed. This discussion would take us a bit off point for the body of this book, but we will look at it in the appendix entitled *The Impossibility of an Infinite Regression*. But for now note that there are a number of excellent writers who have shown that this sort of infinite regress is impossible (see Copan 2001, 64–65; Craig 2008, 96–126 Geisler 1999, 366).

But doesn't everything need a cause? No. The Law of Causality holds that every effect must have a sufficient cause. It does not say that everything *is* an effect. So to ask, "Who made God?" is a category error. You are putting God into the category of the creation, when by definition, that is not what we mean by God. God is not caused. God is the *I AM*.

I actually attempted to explain this in one of those children's sermons mentioned above. It was in response to a question, but it still might have not been my best idea to try to explain this to kids. I asked them, "What makes water wet?" (I know there is discussion about how the chemical makeup of water makes it wet, but that is kind of the point. It is the makeup of water that makes it wet, not any outside force.) Nothing makes water wet; water makes everything else wet. Nothing brings God into being; God brings everything else into being, because God has the power to be.

This analogy, like all analogies, breaks down. Some would say that water isn't wet, it just makes you wet when you touch it. This was just a children's sermon, after all—but then again, what we are saying is that water has the power to make things wet in its very nature. I compared this to how the power to be, and to bring into being, is in God's very nature.

This truth has great implications for our understanding of God and the creation. For one thing, if you have the power to be, then you are by nature eternal. If you are self-existent, you do not cease to be—or, for that matter, begin to be. So Psalm 90:2 tells us,

> Before the mountains were born,
> Or Thou didst give birth to the earth and the world,
> Even from everlasting to everlasting, Thou art God.

Much later, Paul writes to Timothy, "Now to the King eternal, immortal, invisible, the only God, be honor and glory forever and ever" (1 Timothy1:17). Another implication is that God is completely transcendent and yet immanent. Because of God's nature, God is completely beyond the creation—but, because God is the One who has created, he is also deeply involved with the creation.

If all of this is true, then all of existence has meaning. The universe and the world are not random and, as a result, your life is neither meaningless nor random. A God who has the power to exist brought into being all else, with a purpose, and did so intentionally. The God who is eternal has created time for a reason, and therefore our use of the time given to us has meaning. The creation has value, creatures have value, and *you* have value. As Francis Schaeffer said in the title of one of his sermons, *There Are No Little People* (Schaeffer 1972b, 13).

So there is hope, even when we can't see it. This doctrine, which some may consider abstract, is quite practical. (I believe all doctrine is practical.) Your life is intended by God to be important. The One who has the power to exist has brought you into being. You have value as an image-bearer of God. We are all fallen and broken and need repentance and forgiveness. We all need redemption and we are unworthy, but we are not worthless. As Dr. Schaeffer said in the sermon we just mentioned, if God can use a dead stick of wood as he did with Aaron's rod, then God can use you.

It is this great God, this great *I AM*, this One who has the power to exist as part of his very nature, that Jesus claimed to be. By identifying with the name YHWH, and by accepting the worship due only to YHWH, Jesus was claiming to be this God who had become incarnate into the creation. So let's explore just how Jesus claimed to be YHWH.

The Divine Name

Names are important. You are uncomfortable when your name is mispronounced; it's even worse if someone calls you by the wrong name. Your name identifies who you are and even what makes you who you are: your nationality and family background. As we look at the ways in which Jesus claimed to be God, there are actually those who would ask *which* God or god Jesus was claiming to be.

Now, on the surface, this question seems strange. Jesus was a Jew living in Israel. He was the child of a Jewish mother, which is a common definition of being Jewish. He grew up in a Jewish village and attended synagogue and made at least one trip to the temple in Jerusalem as a child. As a teacher, Jesus referred to the Hebrew Scriptures and quoted the prophets. On the day of his death, he quoted from the Psalms. Given all of this, we can be sure Jesus was not claiming to be Thor, or Zeus, or a Flying Spaghetti Monster. Jesus was claiming to be the God of Israel, the God of the Hebrew Scriptures, and the God of Abraham, Isaac, and Jacob.

Most are aware that the name of God is the most highly honored name in Judaism. It is considered too holy to be spoken. Christians may not find warrant for such a view in Scripture itself, but we do honor the commandment not to take the name of God in vain. If Jesus took on that name for himself, it would the highest possible claim to be God. It would identify him specifically with the infinite, omniscient, omnipresent, omnipotent God of the Bible. The historic Christian claim is that Jesus applied the name Yahweh to himself. In doing so, he claimed to be God.

We saw above that, in Exodus 3, God gave his name to Moses. The four letter name— YHWH—is the name Jews do not pronounce. Christians generally pronounce the name Yahweh. In the Bible, it is usually printed as LORD to show the historic respect for the name. I often think it would be good to return to the use of Yahweh in modern translations, to help people regain the personal sense of the God who is speaking. It might help Christians stay clear of a generic view of all gods being the same.

Through all of the Old Testament, Yahweh repeatedly claimed to be the one and only God of all creation. Even if we would just look at the prophet Isaiah we would see a number of examples. In Isaiah 43:10-13, we see Yahweh saying,

> "You are My witnesses," declares the LORD,
> "And My servant who I have chosen,
> In order that you may know and believe Me,
> And understand that I am He
> Before Me there was no God formed,
> And there will be none after me.
> I, even I, am the LORD;
> And there is no savior besides Me."

Then in 44:6-8, again Yahweh is speaking and issues a challenge.

> Thus says the LORD, the King of Israel
> And His Redeemer, the LORD of hosts:
> "I am the first and I am the last,
> And there is no God besides Me.
> And who is like Me? Let him proclaim and declare it;
> Yes, let him recount it to Me in order,
> From the time that I established the ancient nation,
> And let them declare to them the things that are coming
> And the events that are going to take place.
> Do not tremble and do not be afraid.
> Have I not long since announced it to you and declared it?
> And you are My witnesses,
> Is there any God besides Me,
> Or is there any other Rock?
> I know of none."

When Yahweh says, "there is no God besides Me," his meaning is pretty clear. Then he adds, "Is there any God besides Me, Or is there any other Rock? I know of none." When we understand the nature of the God the Bible speaks of, we realize that there can only be one God. Then, just to make sure we do not miss it, Yahweh continues to speak clearly in chapter 45. In verse 14 he says, "Surely, God is with you, and there is none else, No other God." In verse 18, God adds, "I am the LORD, and there is none else." Then the claim goes on in verse 21:

> And there is no other God besides Me,
> A righteous God and a Savior;
> There is none except Me.

And, picking up on the theme of savior, which will be important in the next chapter, Yahweh says in verse 22,

> Turn to Me, and be saved all the ends of the earth;
> For I am God and there is no other.

Jesus Claims to Be YHWH

So Yahweh, the self-existing God of the Old Testament, claims to be the only God. Today, many teach that Jesus did not claim to be *this* God of the Hebrew Bible—but we have evidence that those who were actually in his presence certainly thought that was *exactly* what he was saying. In John 5, we see Jesus healing a man at the Pool of Bethesda on the Sabbath. It was the Passover and Jesus was in Jerusalem, near what was known as the sheep gate. Many would come to the pool called Bethesda to seek healing. Jesus saw a man who had been sick for thirty-eight years. We are not told how Jesus knew he had been ill for a long time, but we are told that he knew. We also are told that Jesus asked what seems to us to be a strange question: "Do you wish to get well?"

We might wonder why Jesus asked this question. Of course the man wanted healed, that is why he was there. But had Jesus seen some sense that the man had given up? Did he think the man might worry that, because he was a beggar, he might have lost his income if he was healed? Perhaps Jesus wanted to see an affirmation from this man that he was really there for the healing and was personally trusting God for it. The man answered by explaining that he had no help to get into the water, which showed that he was, in fact, seeking healing—and so Jesus healed him right there on the spot.

Another layer to the story is revealed when we see that all of this happened on the Sabbath. This caused Jesus to get in trouble for healing on the Sabbath, and the man in trouble for carrying his pallet, since no work could be done on the Sabbath. Some of the witnesses who were there, instead of caring for the man and rejoicing at his healing, sought only to catch Jesus in a doing something wrong. But Jesus said he must be doing what His Father has been doing. Yahweh was still doing acts of kindness and caring, even on the Sabbath—so why should Jesus not do the works of his Father?

The critics took offense at this, and in verse 18 we read, "Therefore the Jews sought all the more to kill Him, because He not only broke the Sabbath, but also said that God was His Father, making Himself equal with God." Those who were in his presence knew he was claiming to be God. Are they not more apt to get it right than critics who are 2000 years removed in time and culture? Notice also that the word used here for "equal" is the Greek word *ison,* which becomes important to us when we look at John 10:30.

In John 10, we see that Jesus was at the temple during the Feast of Dedication. Jesus was walking in the portico of Solomon, when once again he was approached by a number of men who challenged him as to why he simply did not come right out and say he was the Messiah. Jesus said that he had told them and had displayed who he was by his actions, which he claims he did in the name of his Father. We need to notice that Jesus calls God "My Father," which was not normal language for a Jew of his day. It called attention to his claim of a unique connection to Yahweh. Then, as if to build on this idea, he said, "I and the Father are one."

The word for "one" is *en*, which is neuter. This is a preposition in Greek that means a fixed position or a joint state of being. Jesus is not saying he is one in purpose with the Father or even of one mind. Those are certainly both true, but in this context he is saying they are one in being. So here again we see the emphasis being on unity of essence or being. It is perfectly consistent with the claim to be "equal" with God that we saw in John 5. While Jesus certainly shares the desire and will of the Father, the claim here is focused on his essence. They are *the same God*. This has been the Christian position from the beginning, as formalized at the Council of Nicaea. This council focused on the deity of Jesus and not, as some conspiracy theories hold, which books should be included in the Bible. "At the Council of Nicaea, Christian belief as to the Person of Christ was clarified by the insertion into the creedal formula of the word *homoousios* (ie., identity of being with the Father). This has remained a very essential part of the Christian belief. Our Lord is not merely a likeness of the Father, but is 'one substance with the Father'" (Hammond 1973, 96).

In fact, we can be even more specific. In Isaiah 42:8, Yahweh identifies himself by the four-letter name that we have been speaking of: YHWH. Yahweh says, "I am the LORD [YHWH], that is My name; I will not give My glory to another, Nor my praise to graven images." Yahweh says he will not share his glory with anyone.

Again, unless we are willing to claim that Jesus was ignorant of the words of the book of Isaiah, even though he quoted from the book in Luke 4, then we must be amazed at what he says in John 17:5. We have here what is often referred to as the High Priestly Prayer of Jesus. In this prayer, Jesus spoke to God the Father and said, "and now, glorify Thou Me together with Thyself, Father, with the glory which I ever had with Thee before the world was."

The Old Testament Yahweh said he does not share his glory—and yet Jesus claims to have shared in this glory from before the world existed. Therefore, they are one being. Jesus claimed to *be*

Yahweh. He spoke of his own preexistence, and even held that he was not part of the creation but was, in fact, the Creator. This is no veiled claim here; it is clear logic and it provides one example of why the doctrine of the Trinity is so important. There is only one God, Yahweh, and both the Father and the Son are that God. From this we begin to see that a unity in essence and multiplicity of person is possible, and even necessary, in one God. Scripture also clearly shows that this same relationship applies to the Holy Spirit as well.

But do not fall into thinking that what we have said so far is all the evidence there is that Jesus is Yahweh. The pattern we saw in Isaiah 44:6 continues:

> Thus says the LORD, the King of Israel
> And his Redeemer, the LORD of Hosts:
> I am the first and I am the last,
> And there is no God besides Me.

Keeping this in mind we see that the Apostle John wrote that Jesus spoke to him in Revelation, chapter 1. In the midst of symbols from the Old Testament representing the glory, the holiness, and the power of God, Jesus claimed to be the One who is the first and the last; the one spoken of in Isaiah. This is a claim of universal sovereignty. But I am sure some will say that this is a vision and not the historical Jesus, so it does not really count. Well then, let's get back to what the incarnate Jesus said.

In Ezekiel 34, Yahweh promised to be the shepherd of his people and Psalm 23 tells us that "The LORD (Yahweh) is my shepherd." Yet in John 10:11, Jesus identified himself as the good shepherd who shepherds his flock. The caretaker of the people of God found in the Hebrew Bible, the One who will shepherd Israel, the One who will watch over his church—this is the Jesus of the New Testament.

In passages like Joel 3:12 and Genesis 18:25, as well as in many Psalms, we are told that Yahweh is judge of the world. For instance, in Psalm 9:7-8,

> But the LORD (Yahweh) abides forever;
> He has established His throne for judgment,
> And He will judge the world in righteousness;
> He will execute judgment for the peoples with equity.

Yahweh is the judge of the earth, and all that is in it. Yet we see that Jesus, in Matthew 25:31, began to describe how he is the judge who sits on the throne and divides the sheep from the goats. Using his favorite title for himself, Jesus claimed to sit on the throne of Yahweh and offer judgment—an act reserved for Yahweh in the Old Testament. We will see more of this when we look at the attribute of holiness.

Probably the most famous claim of this kind is found in John 8:58. Jesus was being asked by his fellow Jews if he was comparing himself to the greatness of Abraham. He replied that it was *his* coming that Abraham looked forward to. Then he said, "Truly, truly, I say to you, before Abraham was born, I AM." Here Jesus spoke of his preexistence before the days of Abraham and identified himself as the great I Am, Yahweh. Those around him understood once again the power of his claim and picked up stones to take his life, because they considered it blasphemy.

This "I Am" phrase has stirred up some controversy. If you do a search for *I AM*, you will find some very good discussions and some bizarre interpretations. We know that, when the Jews wanted to translate the Hebrew Bible into Greek—so that Jewish readers influenced by the Hellenization of their day could read it—they translated the name of God, YHWH, as *ego eimi*. The word *eimi* on its own can mean *I am* as in "I am going to the bank." It is used this way in Matthew 3:11, Luke 3:16, and other places. But the addition of *ego* adds to the strength of the word (not just *I am* but *I, I am*), and so it was used in the Septuagint (the Greek version of the Hebrew Bible) as the translation of the name of God.

Now what makes this important to what Jesus thought of

himself is that the words used here in John 8:58 to tell us what Jesus said are *ego eimi*. Even if Jesus spoke Aramaic the gospel writers understood Jesus's meaning to be conveyed *ego eimi*, and had him using this phrase frequently, especially in the specific *I AM* passages in the Gospel of John where he used it in every case. Almost without exception, Jesus used this phrase to refer to himself and, as we see in this instance in John, it was not lost on the people in his presence.

All of this means that no other leader or founder of a world religion has claimed for themselves the status Jesus claimed. Jesus demonstrated this in many ways—but the basis is found here in his claim to bear the name of God himself. Buddha said not to look to him, but look to his teaching. Jesus said "Come unto me." Buddha said there is no God; Jesus said "I AM."

Ravi Zacharias makes the point for us.

> Whatever we make of their claims, one reality is inescapable. They are teachers who point to their teaching or show some particular way. In all of these, there emerges an instruction, a way of living. It is not Zoroaster to whom you turn. It is Zoroaster to whom you listen. It is not Buddha who delivers you; it is his Noble Truths that instruct you. It is not Mohammed who transforms you; it is the beauty of the Koran that woos you.

By contrast, Jesus did not only teach and expound His message. He was identical with His message. "In Him," say the Scriptures, "dwelt the fullness of the Godhead bodily." He did not just proclaim the truth. He said, "I am the truth." He did not just show a way. He said, "I am the Way." He did not just open up vistas. He said, "I am the door." "I am the Good Shepherd." "I am the resurrection and the life." "I am the I AM" (Zacharias 2000, 89).

Jesus Claims Pre-Existence

If God is love, then God must exist in something like the Trinity—and if Jesus is God, then we can see why Jesus is seen as the paragon of love. If the Trinity has always been, and Jesus is the second person of that Trinity, then Jesus must have always been. Let's look at the idea of Christophanies (an Old Testament appearance of Christ) and the preexistence of Jesus. Jesus does make this claim for himself.

The first place one thinks of this claim is John 8:57-59. Jesus was having one of his discussions with his fellow Jews of the day in which Jesus made the statement that Abraham was happy to see the day of Jesus. Did this mean that Abraham had a vision, or saw the future? Did he just look ahead by faith to the promises God had made to him concerning a Messiah? Jesus's answer indicates something much more than a vision. The people were questioning him as to how he could know what Abraham experienced. They pointed out that Jesus was not yet even fifty years old. How could he have seen Abraham, who died long before Jesus was born? Jesus responded with the famous line: "Truly, truly, I say to you, before Abraham was born, I AM." Jesus used the *I AM* words that were immediately understood by the Jews to refer to the name of God. They immediately wanted to stone him for blasphemy but, as he often did, he escaped their anger. The claim that Bethlehem was not the beginning of Jesus's existence was clear to the people around him.

Moreover, in Jesus's high priestly prayer in John 17, Jesus prays to the Father in the presence of his disciples. In verse 5, he prays, "Now, Father, glorify Me together with Yourself, with the glory which I had with You before the world was." Here is another affirmation by Jesus that he existed before the incarnation, and in fact, from all eternity.

Some critics claim this idea of pre-existence is found only in John, and so it might have been John's own creation. But Jesus often says—in Matthew, Mark, and Luke—"I have come." In response to the critics Josh and Sean McDowell point to the verses in these gospels and quote Gathercole concerning what the "I have come" statements say about Jesus: "He is seen as having come from somewhere to carry out his life's work, namely, from heaven ... [I]f you read Matthew and Luke carefully in light of their Jewish background, you can see that they have everything to do with Christ existing before he was conceived, before he 'came' to embark on his earthly mission" (Gathercole, 2014, in McDowell and McDowell 2017, 188).

This is not a new understanding of these verses. In 1955, G. C. Berkouwer pointed to the same passages and said,

> Only when a person isolates the "I-have-come" texts from the whole of the Scriptural message, can he deny their deep meaning. But whoever listens without bias to the entire testimony of Scripture will discover in many utterances of the Synoptics the same background which appears so clearly in the gospel of John when he speaks of the great mystery of Christ: He has descended out of heaven (Berkouwer 1954, 167).

Those who followed Jesus picked up on his claims to preexistence and also held to this aspect of his deity. Jesus's claim to eternality would necessarily mean his preexistence. This is certainly how Paul spoke of Jesus in the second chapter of Philippians, where Paul may be quoting an earlier Christian hymn, which would make this belief an even earlier affirmation of the church. These verses speak of a Jesus who had an existence as God prior to the incarnation, but he did not hold onto that position; instead, he emptied himself to be as one of us. This is clearly a movement in time and makes no sense without Jesus's preexistence. It is not about Jesus trying to be like God but is, in fact, just the opposite. This passage teaches that

Jesus once had that equality with God, and he gave up that right so he could be incarnate.

Jesus was born in this world. His human life had a beginning—but his divine nature is from all eternity. It is this preexistence that John depends on when he points out the difference between Jesus and the prophets of the Old Testament. John tells us that Jesus is different because he does not just receive a word from God, but comes from God and reveals God to us in a way only a member of the Trinity could. "No one has seen God at any time; the only begotten God who is in the bosom of the Father, He has explained Him" (John 1:18).

Jesus Accepts Worship

It has been said that a teacher wants the student to learn what the teacher knows. In addition, a Christian teacher wants the student to become what the teacher is: a disciple of Christ. The role of a guru is to lead and guide and offer directions along the way of life. Jesus claimed to be much more than a guru showing the way: he claimed to *be* the Way. He is the object of worship—worship he knew was due only to God.

Theologian Charles Hodge describes how Jesus was the object of worship for the Apostles and the early church:

> Christ is the God of the Apostles and early Christians, in the sense that He is the object of all their religious affections. They regarded Him as the person to whom they specially belonged; to whom they were responsible for their moral conduct; to whom they had to account for their sins; for the use of their time and talents; who was ever present with them, dwelling in them, controlling their inward, as well as their outward life; whose love was the animating principle of their being; in

whom they rejoiced as their present joy and as their
everlasting portion (Hodge 1997, 1:498).

Once again, we must remember that Jesus was a Jew. He knew
that, as did all his fellow Jews, the Hebrew Bible teaches clearly that
only God is to be worshiped. This is a foundational belief for the
Jews and strongly stated in the first few verses of Exodus 20 as God
gives the Ten Commandments. Those Ten Commandments start
with a powerful and clear call to worship no one but Yahweh, to
put nothing in his place, and to honor even his name. Jesus himself
acknowledges this belief when being challenged by Satan during
Jesus' temptation. In Matthew 4 Jesus had just been baptized and
was taken out into the wilderness by the Holy Spirit where, after
a physical trial of hunger and thirst, he was tempted by Satan.
In Matthew 4:10, Jesus responded to the temptation by quoting
Scripture and pointing out that only God is to be worshiped.

So it was Jesus's own belief and teaching that only God is to
be worshiped. By God, Jesus was referring to YHWH, the God
of the Old Testament. Yet it is amazing that Jesus did not rebuke
those who offered to him worship and honor due only to God.
In the book of Matthew, we see a number of occasions on which
Jesus accepted worship. On one occasion, Jesus had just finished
the Sermon on the Mount and came down the mountain from that
event with a great crowd of people following him. In Matthew 8:2,
we read, "And behold, a leper came to Him, and bowed down to
him, saying, 'Lord, if You are willing, You can make me clean.'"
The word *bowed* is also translated *worship* or *worshipped* forty-nine
times in the New American Standard Bible (Thomas 1981, 1679).

The word *bowed* carries along with it the meaning of giving
reverence to someone or something. Jesus offered no rebuke for
this act of worship but, instead of turning him away, he touched
the leper—and healed him. As a result, instead of Jesus being
made ceremonially unclean (as would normally be the case when
touching a leper), Jesus's touch made the leper physically clean.

Then in Matthew 9:18, the same word is used when a synagogue official came to Jesus and again bowed down in worship, asking for Jesus's help in raising his daughter from the dead. The man was seeking Jesus's physical touch for the girl, and after a brief interruption, Jesus brought that healing. Healing is usually the focus here but we must also notice that Jesus accepted the act of worship with no rebuke.

In Matthew 14:33, Jesus had just walked on the water, and the result was what we might expect: the apostles worshiped him. They saw Jesus walking on the water and then they saw Peter go out to meet him as Jesus challenged Peter's faith. Then, as Peter and Jesus got into the boat, the apostles worshiped Jesus, claiming him to be God's Son. It is in that powerful context that Jesus challenged their lack of faith—and yet we notice again that he did not challenge their worshiping attitude toward him.

Not long after this event we see, in Matthew 15:25, a Canaanite woman who was desperate to find help for her daughter. She came and fell in worship at the feet of Jesus. The unusual response of Jesus raises questions for some people. Jesus reminded the woman that she was not a Jew and that he had come first for the lost house of Israel. It is that context of priorities that Jesus said, in verse 26, "It is not good to take the children's bread and throw it to the dogs."

Some think Jesus was being somewhat rude here, but the language is that of a pet dog and a family setting. Jesus was not calling her daughter a dog. In fact, the woman understood the proverb and said that she would even accept crumbs. In this incident, Jesus's response was once again compassion for the daughter with no hint of rebuke for the act of worship. Some might say that all of these events just show a humble Jesus not wanting to rebuke these good folks, but accommodating them so as not to hurt their feelings. To be sure, Jesus was humble—but humility is not humility unless there is actual ability behind it. If I do not flaunt my golfing abilities, that would not be humility, because my golfing is not great; but if Phil Mickelson did not flaunt his abilities, that would be humility.

Jesus was not merely being humble. He was tacitly admitting who he was by living it out, by healing, by raising the dead, and by acting as one worthy of worship.

The mother of the apostles who were called the sons of Zebedee came to Jesus in Matthew 20:20 and worshiped him, even as she made a request that showed she did not quite get the whole Kingdom of God idea just yet. The request for her boys (James and John) did not sit too well with the other apostles, and even Jesus reminded her that she did not quite know what she was asking. Yet Jesus again accepted her worship just as he did after the resurrection, when the women came from the empty tomb and encountered Jesus (Matthew 28:29). The women reacted as we might expect when, having just seen the empty tomb, they then come face to face with Jesus. They ran to him and fell down and worshiped him. Jesus did not attempt to stop the worship, but instead told them to go and tell others what they had seen. They did exactly as Jesus said, and when the apostles heard the news from the women they came to Jesus and worshiped him also (verse 17).

Just to be clear, Jesus's attitude toward being worshiped is not a theme only in Matthew. In Mark 5:6, we are told of a man with an unclean spirit that made him wild and self-destructive. "And seeing Jesus from a distance, he ran up and bowed down before Him." The man displayed an act of worship while the demon in him rebelled. Yet Jesus set the man free and fully accepted the act of worship.

The Gospel of John tells us more. In John 9 we see that Jesus healed a man who had been born blind. The Pharisees were angry because all of this took place on the Sabbath and they did not want to believe the man's testimony. Jesus challenged the man's faith, and in verse 38, the man's response was to profess belief in Jesus and to offer worship. Once again, Jesus had some hard words for the Pharisees—but no criticism for the man who worshiped him.

Another act of worship—or we might say a call to worship—happens in the Gospel of John. Is prayer not an act of worship? Prayer is at least a part of worship. When Jesus said we are to pray to him and in his name, was he not confessing his own deity? In

John 1:13-14, Jesus said, "And whatever you ask in My name, that will I do, that the Father may be glorified in the Son. If you ask Me anything in My name, I will do it." Did Jesus claim to be God? He accepted worship and called on us to pray to him. That would seem to be a clear claim.

Today, we might hear that the early church invented the claim that Jesus is God, but that charge does not seem to stand up to Jesus's own claims to be YHWH and to even accept the worship due only to YHWH. Yet this is only the first of the attributes of God we are going to see in Jesus. This is one more way the charge that the early church invented the deity of Jesus runs into some problems, as G.C. Berkouwer pointed out:

> From the preceding it is plain that the question of Christ as the Son of God, indeed, as himself truly God, is charged, already in Jesus's lifetime, with the awful seriousness of final decisions; and that Christ has been mocked and tempted on account of his claim. This is all the more striking because later on this seriousness was quite lost at times. Christ's deity is then interpreted as a creation of the infant church which more and more endowed Jesus of Nazareth with divine attributes. The Jews took another direction. They accused Christ himself of this creation, of this deification. "He made himself the Son of God" (John 19:7). Their testimony, annoyance, criticism, and opposition, with all its consequences, point to the clarity with which Christ made his claim. Theirs was not a misunderstanding which Christ, to avoid the worst, could have eliminated, but theirs was the seriousness of an ultimate decision, the decision regarding life and death. How plain is here the inseparable union of the person with the work of

Christ! In the self-testimony of Christ, he who died outside the gates of Jerusalem for blasphemy, the two confront as a unity (Berkouwer 1954, 173).

Apostolic Testimony

As we look at some of the attributes of God that Jesus claimed to possess, it might also be helpful to see how the apostles viewed these attributes and how they, from the earliest days, made the connection that Jesus bore the attributes of divinity. The claim that Jesus was the God of the Hebrew Bible was not an invention of a later generation of faith.

We might not notice the statement made by Paul in 1 Timothy 6:15, because the language is so familiar. Paul challenges believers in the name of God and of Jesus Christ and refers to God as, "He who is the blessed and only Sovereign, the King of Kings and Lord of lords." Now this title certainly looks back to the description of God in Deuteronomy 10:17, "For the LORD your God is the God of Gods and Lord of lords, the great, the mighty, and the awesome God who does not show partiality, nor take a bribe." What is striking about this language is that it is also used twice in Revelation in reference to Jesus (17:14; 19:16) which, as Donald Guthrie points out, tells us that the title was already "an accepted Christian ascription" for Jesus by the time Revelation was written. So we see the sovereignty of Yahweh attributed to Jesus (Guthrie 1976, 116).

But all of this is just the beginning. In Psalm 24:7-10, we read that God, Yahweh, is the King of Glory, the Lord almighty:

Lift up your heads, O gates,
And be lifted up, O ancient doors,
That the King of Glory may come in!
Who is the King of Glory?
The LORD strong and mighty,

> The LORD mighty in battle.
> Lift up your heads, O gates,
> And lift them up, O ancient doors,
> That the King of glory may come in!
> Who is this King of glory?
> The LORD of hosts,
> He is the King of glory.

Does it not seem that, to use the term *Lord of glory* or *King of glory* in a Jewish context, one would be speaking of the LORD/Yahweh of this passage? It might well be that no one in the first century knew the Hebrew Bible better than Paul. Yet in 1 Corinthians 2:8, Paul says that the people of this age "crucified the Lord of glory" because they did not understand the wisdom of God. Jesus is the Lord of Glory and God (Yahweh) is the King of Glory. It seems clear that Jesus is identified with the Yahweh of Psalm 24.

Peter talks of Jesus as a cornerstone in 1 Peter 2:7, which ties Jesus to Psalm 118:22. Even more directly, Peter takes this image and, in 1 Peter 2:8, identifies it with Isaiah 8:13-14 which says;

> It is the LORD of hosts whom you should regard
> as holy.
> And He shall be your fear,
> And He shall be your dread.
> Then He shall become a sanctuary;
> But to both the houses of Israel, a stone to strike
> and a rock to stumble over,
> And a snare and a trap for the inhabitants of
> Jerusalem.

In Isaiah, it is Yahweh who is this stone and rock to stumble over—but Peter makes it clear that this also refers to Jesus. It is Yahweh, but it is Jesus; the two cannot be separated. In Isaiah 40:3, we see a call to, "Clear the way for the LORD in the wilderness;

Make smooth in the desert a highway for our God." The way is to be cleared for Yahweh—yet in Matthew 3:3, we see this verse applies to John the Baptist, who is clearing the way for Jesus. For Matthew, Jesus is the Yahweh that they were preparing to receive and the one for whom John the Baptist was preparing the way.

It is also interesting that, just a few verses later in Isaiah 40, this same Yahweh is referred to as a shepherd for his people. Not only is Jesus repeatedly spoken of as a shepherd and, as we saw above, even refers to himself as the Good Shepherd, but the author of Hebrews calls Jesus "the great Shepherd of the sheep" (13:20), directly connecting Jesus to the shepherd of Isaiah 40.

Speaking of shepherds, Jeremiah 23 speaks of God raising up shepherds for his people. But then God makes a bold promise in verses 5 and 6:

> 'Behold the days are coming,' declares the LORD,
> 'When I shall raise up for David a righteous Branch
> And He will reign as king and act wisely
> And do justice and righteousness in the land.
> In His days Judah will be saved,
> And Israel will dwell securely,
> And this is His name by which He will be called,
> The LORD our righteousness.'

We are told that Yahweh will be our righteousness when this Messiah, this righteous Branch comes. This might be exactly what Paul was pointing out when he referred to Jesus as our righteousness in 1Corinthians 1:30.

As we see these connections to Yahweh spoken of in the Psalms and by the prophets of the Old Testament, we also see a general reminder of this connection by Peter. In 1 Peter 1:10-12, Peter speaks of the prophets and claims that they prophesied of the grace that would come. He says that, in their prophesying, they paid close attention to the "Spirit of Christ within them." The Spirit within them in their day was the Spirit of Yahweh. This Spirit is the Spirit of Christ; the Holy Spirit. It was this Spirit of Christ that was active in the Old Testament prophets. This Spirit, who comforted and empowered the incarnate Jesus, is the Holy Spirit. It is the Spirit of Jesus, of Yahweh. The claim is that they are the one and the same God.

The foundation of all that we want to look at is that the God of the Bible, the God of historic Christianity, is an independent God. God is a being who, by his very nature, has the power to be and gives being to all other things. It is therefore appropriate that the name this God chooses for himself is *I Am* or Yahweh. It is this God Jesus was referring to when he claimed to be God. It is this name he connected with and identified with when he accepted the worship of others. It is this God and this name that the apostles attributed to Jesus himself as they acknowledged his deity.

CHAPTER THREE

▼

THE CLAIM TO BE MESSIAH

IN THE INTRODUCTION, we talked about people who want to say, "My God is a God of love." They speak as if the attributes of God could be divided, or as if somehow God cannot be justice and holiness and love at the same time. Some people act as though love, whatever their concept of that may be, is all there is to God. While we cannot affirm that love is all there is to God, we cannot deny that the Bible makes it clear that the love of God is of great importance.

The verse most often mentioned in this context is 1 John 4:8, "The one who does not love does not know God, for God is love." Saying that God is love is one thing—but many have tried to reverse this statement so that God becomes merely a feeling or a concept and not a real Being who, by his nature, is love. You cannot just reverse the phrase *God is love* and make it *love is God*. It is a logical error to reverse a statement like this. *The sky is blue* does not also mean that blue is the sky. Lots of other things are blue. *The car is red* does not mean that red is a car. I have six red things on my desk, and they are not cars, they are paper clips. *God is love* does not mean that love is God, even if that gives some in our generation a good feeling.

None the less, God is a loving and good Being. These attributes are significant because it is the goodness and love of God that brings Jesus to us as the Messiah. While the goodness and love of God might not be attributes Jesus speaks about possessing, he does live them out constantly, and he does speak about being the Messiah. Since it is these attributes that lay the foundation for a Messiah to come, we need to look at them before we see Jesus's claims to be this Messiah—and then see that the claim to be Messiah is a claim to be divine.

The Biblical worldview tells us that the reason God created human beings as personal is that God exists as personal. It is in this way that we are image bearers of God. Human beings then rebelled against God and fell from their relationship with God. If God is a God of love and of goodness, would it not seem to follow that God would desire to heal that broken relationship? The whole of Scripture is about the plan to bring that healing through the incarnation of the Messiah, coming to pay the cost of the evil done by humanity and each individual that makes up humanity. It is a plan based on God's love and goodness.

When we speak of the love of God, we are talking partly about God's patience. This is what Peter was talking about in 2 Peter 3:9: "The Lord is not slow about His promise, as some count slowness, but is patient toward you, not wishing for any to perish but for all to come to repentance." God, in his love, holds back judgment even when his people rebel against him. For instance, when Adam and Eve sinned, they did die spiritually that day, just as had been promised, but they did not die physically so that they might have opportunity to repent. Many people are bothered by the taking of Canaan by the Israelites and God's calling for the destruction of the people who lived there, but this is actually an example of God's patience. We need to see that, after they heard the teaching of Abraham, God gave the people in that land more than four centuries to come to faith in Yahweh (Genesis 15:16; Exodus 12:40; Leviticus 18:24-30). The Canaanites practiced child sacrifice, polytheism, religious prostitution, and much more—yet God gave them more than four centuries to listen to the word that had been given to them.

Truth be told, God is long-suffering with all of us. Even as we hope for the return of Jesus, God is not slow, but patient for our sake. When dealing with the problem of evil, God's patience causes some to ask why God does not just zap evil out of existence. But if God did so, who among us would be left? In what turns out to be a blessing for us, God in his love is *not* zapping evil. He is redeeming it and allowing us to be part of his plan for redemption as we share the good news.

This patience also shows us how mercy is a part of God's love. When God acts with compassion directed at his creatures we see his mercy. James 5:11 tells us, "Behold, we count those blessed who endured. You have heard of the endurance of Job and have seen the outcome of the Lord's dealings, that the Lord is full of compassion and is merciful." Compassion means to be *with suffering,* which is what God promises us. In this broken world, God does not promise to remove us, because we are part of the brokenness. God promises to be with us in the brokenness. His presence with us is his mercy. The prophet Isaiah tells us as much:

> For He said, "Surely, they are My people,
> Sons who will not deal falsely."
> So He became their Savior.
> In all their affliction He was afflicted
> And the angel of His presence saved them;
> In His love and in His mercy He redeemed them;
> And He lifted them and carried them all the days
> of old (Isaiah 63:8-9).

Closely related to God's love shown in mercy is God's love shown in grace. If mercy is the offering of God's love based on compassion, then grace is the offering of God's love to those who do not deserve it—and that would be all of us. Often the mercy and grace of God are seen as being in conflict with the justice of God. The love of God and the justice of God do not seem to match up for some people. If God imposes justice, they seem to feel that somehow God is not being loving. But the question is, how much do you love someone if you do not act justly against the evil that is oppressing them or stand against the person who is harming them? Justice is love because it protects the innocent and prevents the wicked from becoming more wicked.

Some ask, "Why doesn't God just forgive the evil?" Why is God not just a nice, forgiving, soft-hearted Being who just lets things slide? Because there is a cost to evil. Evil is real, and it really hurts people. If there were no consequences to evil in the order of God's creation and Kingdom, then God would be evil.

I heard Josh McDowell one time in a seminar at the Creation Festival use the illustration of a boy bouncing a basketball in the house. (It was not part of Josh's illustration, but I always seem to picture Beaver and Mr. Cleaver when I think of this.) The father had told the boy not to bounce the ball in the living room, but he disobeyed and bounced it anyway and broke a lamp. Now the father could have considered any number of things and not disciplined the boy. He could have forgiven him for whatever reason. The boy could be truly forgiven and off the hook for punishment, because of his father's forgiveness, though that would be a bit of a stretch in most homes.

And yet, even if the father gives his son blanket forgiveness a question still exists, who pays for the lamp? If evil is real, and real damage and hurt occur, then both love and justice would demand that some payment be made. Justice would call for a response, a recompense. The good news is that, if we seek God's forgiveness, God's mercy and grace are there for us because Jesus paid the price.

It is also good news that when no forgiveness is sought, justice is also a part of the nature, and even the love, of God. There is no conflict between requiring that there be a payment for evil and the notion that God is love. Justice is sure, and justice is a part of God's goodness, but we are grateful that God might go beyond justice and offer mercy (though God is never guilty of injustice).

When we describe the goodness of God it is often spoken of in general terms in the sense that something is good when it is perfect in all of its parts. It is true that part of God's goodness is that God is completely, internally consistent. God is in every way, what we mean when we say *good*. This definition of goodness has to do with not only morality but with absolute perfection. We only know God as he reveals himself, and we only know a God who cares for, and does good things for, his creatures.

This is why, in discussing both God's love and his goodness, we can say that God shows a general goodness toward all of his creatures. Matthew 5:45 tells us that God causes "His sun to rise on the evil and the good, and sends rain on the righteous and the unrighteous." Jesus affirms this in Matthew 6:26: "Look at the birds of the air, that they do not sow, neither do they reap, nor gather into barns, and yet your heavenly Father feeds them. Are you not worth much more than they?" The psalmist also tells us:

> Sing to the LORD with thanksgiving;
> Sing praises to our God on the lyre,
> Who covers the heavens with clouds,
> Who provides rain for the earth,
> Who makes grass to grow on the mountains.
> He gives to the beast its food,
> And to the young ravens which cry (Psalm 147:7-9).

So God's general goodness is directed at all of creation. One of the most frequent questions that arises when defending the Christian faith these days is the problem of evil and suffering.

When I attempt to offer a theodicy—an attempt to vindicate God's goodness and justice in the face of evil—I often ask, just to set the stage, "Is there more evil or more goodness in the world?" I've been surprised how often people will say there is more evil than good. Sometimes they add, "Just look at the news." But then I point out a shooting is newsworthy because all the other people in that town did not get shot. The reason the house fire was news is that all the other houses did not burn. The reason the four-car pile-up was on the news is that all the other cars got home safely. The goodness of God can be seen in the creation and the way the world functions, even in its fallen state.

God's goodness also shows in the love he directs toward his rational creatures. This is the foundation for revelation and the communication of God as he makes himself known to us, both in the creation and in Scripture. This goodness is specially shown to those who trust him, but it is also a general love to all those created in his image.

For example, we do not often think about it, but do you realize that God did not have to make food taste good? He did not have to create the beauty in a sunset or in a mountain range. God did not have to make the universe orderly and knowable. These are gifts from the love and goodness of God to all rational creatures. That we can know and observe beauty and order is also evidence that we were created to be in this setting, to exist in this world. This gives the Christian a foundation for knowledge.

Theologian Francis Schaeffer saw this as central to the overall Christian answer to philosophical questions raised in epistemology (Schaeffer 1972a, 37ff.) We, as image bearers of God, were created to experience beauty, to find the world around us fascinating, and to want to seek to understand it. And when Anglican theologian E. A. Litton first published his *Introduction to Dogmatic Theology,* in the late 1800s, he said it is evident that:

> All the contrivances of nature have the well-being and happiness of the whole for their *natural*

tendency; if the aim is not attained, it is in *spite* of the natural arrangements and because they are thwarted by some antagonist power. We never discover a train of contrivance to bring about an evil purpose. If God had been indifferent to our happiness. He might have made, or permitted a rival Power to make, everything we tasted bitter, everything we saw loathsome, everything we touched a sting, every smell a stench, and every sound a discord (Litton 1960, 71).

It is this God who is goodness and compassion; he could not do otherwise than act to save the people he loves. As we will see (and as we saw above in Isaiah 63), the Old Testament tells us that it is the goodness of God that establishes Yahweh as the Savior, Redeemer, and Messiah. It is that Messiah Jesus claims to be.

Messiah as Divine

To have someone say that you have a messiah complex is generally not a compliment. It means you think too much of yourself; you overvalue your importance and think others need you to save them. Someone is saying that you are suffering from an overinflated ego. Some time ago, my wife and I watched *Lawrence of Arabia*, a film we had not seen in many years. It was not what we had remembered. Lawrence was a man with a messiah complex. In one scene, he traveled from Aqaba to Cairo across the Sinai, assuming he could do it because "Moses did." Then, in the middle of what appeared at first to be an attempt to help others, his actions were questioned and his indignant response was, "Do you think I am just any man?" Now there was a big ego. Leaders of all kinds are derided if it appears they think they are some kind of messianic figure superior to the common folk. It is meant to be a criticism simply because we know that none of us have any real claim on being the Messiah. So did Jesus claim to be the Messiah and, if he did, what was he claiming?

The messianic hope of Israel was a positive, God-given hope that came through the prophets. It was a hope that God himself would provide for them, and all the world, an ultimate way of forgiveness. Jesus claimed to be that person: that way of forgiveness. His followers also held him to be that Messiah. However, we need to see that there is a bit more to this Messiah idea than we might think. The messianic hope found in the Old Testament is more than a little complicated. It is not a simple image, but it does include one notion that is important for our purposes in this book: the concept of Messiah includes the understanding that the Messiah will be divine: God (Yahweh) himself will be the Messiah.

Now we need to be careful here. As J. Gresham Machen pointed out a century ago in *The Person of Jesus* (Machen 2016), we are not saying that the prophets of the Old Testament knew clearly that the Messiah was to be one of the persons of the Trinity. But we do see that Yahweh claimed to be the One doing the saving.

As with prophecy in general, hindsight usually makes things clearer. God might give messages in prophecy that contain more than even the prophet understands. Looking back on the prophecy from the perspective of the fulfillment enables believers to connect the fulfillment with the prophecy, and sometimes see more than the prophet saw. The connections we are about to look at were not merely made by modern evangelicals; some appear in the New Testament itself. So even if the authors and prophets of the Old Testament did not always think of Messiah in terms of divinity, that truth is still revealed in the text and fulfilled in Jesus.

If you do a word search through lexicons, concordances, and Bible dictionaries you will find that the word *Messiah* only appears twice (if that) in the Old Testament. Yet, even with that being true, the idea of Messiah and Savior runs all through the prophets. For those who are new to this kind of discussion, it might be helpful to remember that the title *Messiah* is a synonym for *Savior* and that *Christ* is the Greek word for *Messiah* or *anointed one*. Christ is not Jesus's last name, it is a title. So references to a savior in the Old Testament give us a clue to the promise of a Messiah. Let's look at some of the passages that tell us of the Messiah/Savior who was to come.

It has been pointed out that, even in what is possibly the oldest book of the Old Testament, Job seemed to see the need for one who was both human and divine to mediate between God and God's creatures (Job 9:33). The New American Standard Bible has a unique way of translating the verse. Job, speaking to God, admitted,

> There is no umpire between us,
> Who may lay his hand upon us both.

Job realized his separation from God and also realized the need for a mediator, an umpire: someone who could touch both God and man. But to touch God is not something a creature could do. This mediator would need to be divine.

The Messiah, mediator, is depicted often in Scripture as the One who will display a kind of power, authority, and glory that no human Davidic king could have—even though the Davidic kingship is a type of the Messiah to come. We see it in the second Psalm. Yahweh speaks and says that there is to be a King, a Son, who will act in ways no human king could manage. His rule will be universal. This Messianic Son is to be given honor and submission.

> Do homage to the Son, lest He become angry, and
> you perish in the way,
> For His wrath may soon be kindled.
> How blessed are all who take refuge in Him!
> (Psalm 2:12).

Then there is Isaiah 7:14, a verse we hear often at Christmas time. It reminds us that the Messiah who is coming will be both a descendant of David and the presence of God. "Therefore the Lord Himself will give you a sign. Behold, a virgin shall be with child and bear a son, and she will call His name Immanuel." To be sure, this prophecy might have had a connection to what was going on in Isaiah's day and an immediate fulfillment then, though the more I study it, the less I am inclined to this position. Even with that debate in the background, there are a couple of things that are important to us. The first is that the name Immanuel means *God with us*. The ultimate fulfillment of this prophecy would be that the Messiah would be the presence of God with us. Matthew 1:20-23 makes this direct connection to Jesus and affirms that Jesus is Immanuel. He is *God with us*.

Another verse that speaks of the coming Messiah is Isaiah 9:6. It is also a verse we often hear at Christmas, because it is commonly understood to speak of the Messiah, and is seen as being fulfilled in the child Jesus. The verse includes the statement that this Messiah child, "will be called Wonderful Counselor, Mighty God, Eternal Father, Prince of Peace."

Here we see again that this Messiah, the Savior who is to come, will be called *God* and that there is a direct identification with *Eternal Father*. The next verse reminds us that this one who will be coming will be a descendant of David, and all through Isaiah, we see a recurring image of the one who is to come and be greater than David ever was. As we see in the next verse in Isaiah 9, this greater David will be more than human: his kingdom will never end.

> There will be no end to the increase of His
> government or of peace,
> On the throne of David and over his kingdom,
> To establish it and to uphold it with justice and
> righteousness
> From then on and forevermore.
> The zeal of the LORD of hosts will accomplish this.

At this point, we might also want to read the prayer in Psalm 72 that was seen by both later Judaism and the early church as a prayer for the Messiah, this greater Davidic King. This Messiah will be a judge of the earth, a crusher of the oppressor, and a King of kings, whose name will endure forever.

Returning to the prophet Isaiah, we see in 43:11 that Yahweh had just stated that there is no other God besides him, and then goes on to say there is no savior besides him: "I, even I, am the LORD; And there is no savior besides Me."

All of these verses speak of the Messiah as One with divine attributes. This is made even clearer in the next chapter of Isaiah, when Yahweh continues to speak through Isaiah and reaffirms that he is the one and only God, and yet refers to a Redeemer who is also God. As we saw in chapter one, both of the words *LORD* in this verse are the name *Yahweh*. In Isaiah 44:6, Yahweh says:

> Thus says the LORD, the King of Israel
> And his Redeemer, the LORD of hosts:
> I am the first and I am the last,
> And there is no God besides me.

Even as this applies to the redemption of Israel out of Egypt, it also tells us there is no Redeemer, no Messiah, no Savior, except Yahweh. God is the first and the last, the only God. From the perspective of the prophet, when the Redeemer comes, that Redeemer will be Yahweh.

The sense of Yahweh's eternality that we see in these passages becomes prominent in another familiar prophecy, often read at Christmas, that tells us where the Messiah is to be born. Micah 5:2 also reveals a bit about the Messiah's nature:

> But as for you, Bethlehem Ephrathah,
> Too little to be among the clans of Judah,

From you One will come forth for Me to be ruler
in Israel.
His goings forth are from long ago,
From the days of eternity.

The Messiah will come from Bethlehem. The Messiah will be
the One who is eternal. What does this tell us about Jesus? Who
but God is eternal?

Jesus Accepts the Title of Messiah

The average Jew in the first century might not have expected that
the Messiah would be God, but we are concerned here with what
the Scriptures actually said and promised—not what was expected.
Our claim is that, from the beginning, it was part of the biblical
expectation that the Messiah would be divine. "From the nature
of the work which He was to accomplish, it was necessary that He
should be at once God and Man. He must participate in the nature
of those whom He came to redeem; and yet have the power to
subdue all evil, and to give value to his obedience and sufferings"
(Hodge 1997, 1:483).

This has been true from the very first promise of a redeemer
made by God in Genesis 3. The Messiah, the Redeemer, would be
a descendant of Eve and, as such, fully human. Yet the Messiah also
would have the power to overcome Satan and ultimately defeat him
forever, and so would be fully divine.

If the Messiah was to be God—and even if Jesus claimed to be
the Messiah only a few times—his claim would still carry much
weight. One place this is plain is in Mark 14. Jesus was at his trial,
standing before the high priest, who asked a very pointed question:
"Are you the Christ, the Son of the Blessed One?"

We have already noted that *Christ* means *Messiah;* but it is also
the case that the phrase *Blessed One* was used as one of the ways to

avoid saying the name of God. So Jesus was being asked if he was the Messiah, the Son of God. His answer was "I am." The meaning of this answer was clear enough to those standing there that the high priest ripped his clothes as a sign of grief and charged Jesus with blasphemy. Those present knew he was claiming to be God, right there in their presence. It might not be part of our thinking these days, but blasphemy is an affront to the majesty of God. It is a challenge to God's authority. Those who stood there in the presence of Jesus must have understood he was claiming to be God, since they condemned him for a blasphemy worthy of death. The point is, he made the claim, and they knew he made the claim. How do some today deny that Jesus did so?

In Luke 24:25-27, we see an event that took place after the resurrection. It is Jesus' famous appearance on the road to Emmaus. The resurrected Jesus met a couple of his followers along the road on the way to the town of Emmaus. They were having a discussion about all that had gone on in the previous days concerning the crucifixion, and now even word of the resurrection had reached them. But they did not recognize Jesus. Maybe they did not recognize Jesus because they did not expect to see him there. Many of us have that problem when we see people out of context. Or maybe, since the text says that "their eyes were prevented from recognizing him" (verse 16), this was intentional, so that Jesus could share with them the good news of who he was. At any rate, Jesus asked them why they looked sad, and they told him about the happenings of the last couple of days. "And He said to them, 'O foolish men and slow of heart to believe in all that the prophets have spoken! Was it not necessary for the Christ to suffer these things and to enter into His glory?' And beginning with Moses and with all the prophets, He explained to them the things concerning Himself in all the Scriptures."

Jesus showed these early followers that he was the Messiah, according to the Scriptures. He spoke clearly of how Moses and the prophets had foretold his arrival, and how he had now fulfilled their words by coming as the promised Messiah. He then revealed himself to them as they were able to recognize him when he broke bread with them, and their eyes were then opened to see who he truly was. Jesus, in effect, did what this book is attempting to do: He showed how he was and is the Messiah from the claims of the Hebrew Scriptures, the Old Testament.

Some might say this is reading into the Old Testament something that is really a New Testament way of looking at Biblical history. Such a concern is valid, but it would certainly seem that Jesus set the precedent in this passage for just such a reading. Following his example would seem to be a good idea.

We find another example in John 4:25-26. Jesus was having a discussion with the woman at the well. Jesus had challenged her faith, and we see her response in verse 25: "I know that the Messiah is coming (He who is called Christ); when that One comes He will declare all things to us." Then Jesus—holding nothing back at this point—affirmed that he was the Messiah. "I who speak to you am He."

Some speculate that Jesus felt comfortable making this claim to this particular woman since they were in Samaria, where it might not have been as much of a political statement as it would be in Jerusalem. But one way or the other, he made the claim. It carried with it the full weight of what the woman expected. Since, as happened on the road to Emmaus, Jesus was referring to the Old Testament teaching and not merely the expectation of his own day. He was claiming to be that divine Messiah incarnate.

These three claims of Jesus are clear. Do not fall into the trap of thinking that it is not a strong case just because Jesus only self-identified as Messiah three times. First of all, his claiming to be the Messiah is only part of the overall case being made in these chapters. But the argument that Jesus only made the claim three times raises a question. How many times would Jesus have to say it for it to be true? Repeating a statement does not add to the truth it carried the first time it was uttered. It might be the case that, in much of Israel, making this claim would have created more of a political stir than was good for Jesus's mission early on. Yet despite this threat, he did make the affirmation.

Apostolic Testimony

The apostolic witnesses of the New Testament reveal the claim that Jesus was the Messiah in both general and very specific ways. We see this in the connection made in John 19:37 to Zechariah 12:10. In Zechariah 12, Yahweh is speaking of the coming day when enemies shall rise against Israel, but God will defend her and send One who will come from the house of David like an angel of the LORD to defend them. As in many prophecies, the first and second comings of Jesus are seen as one event. Remember Yahweh is speaking, and he promises in verse 10: "And I will pour out on the house of David and on the inhabitants of Jerusalem, the Spirit of grace and of supplication, so that they will look on Me whom they have pierced, and they will mourn for Him, as one mourns for an only son, and they will weep bitterly over Him, like the bitter weeping over a first-born." Yahweh talks of the one who will be pierced but refers to that one as *Me*. This Messiah, this *only son* and *first-born* comes from Yahweh—but is also identified as Yahweh.

This is exactly what John saw when he claimed that this passage, and all that it said about Messiah, was speaking of Jesus. In referring to the crucifixion of Jesus, John claimed it was a fulfilment of Scripture, including this passage from Zechariah: "And again another Scripture says, 'They shall look on Him whom they have pierced.'" John did this again in Revelation 1:7, where he referenced the passage from Zechariah and proclaimed that the One who was spoken of by Yahweh as "Me"—the one who is from David's house—is Jesus.

Paul is also not one to hold back, and in Philippians 2:10-11 he connects Jesus to the words of Isaiah. In Isaiah 45:22, Yahweh claimed to be the savior and the only God, and then went on to make a claim we see again in Philippians. God had already made the claim in verse 21 to be the only God and the savior, and then goes on to say;

> Turn to Me and be saved, all the ends of the earth;
> For I am God and there is no other.
> I have sworn by Myself,
> The word has gone forth from My mouth in righteousness
> And will not turn back. That to Me every knee will
> bow, every tongue will swear allegiance.

Paul then claimed these attributes (Savior and God) for Jesus when he said "at the name of Jesus every knee should bow, of those who are in heaven, and on earth, and under the earth, and that every tongue should confess that Jesus Christ is lord, to the glory of God the Father." Paul used the title "Christ" (Messiah) for Jesus but also made a connection between Jesus and the very nature and being of God found as described in Isaiah.

Peter had already made this claim about the deity of Jesus while Jesus was still with the apostles. In Matthew 16:16, Jesus had just finished the feeding of the four thousand and had a bit of a debate with the Pharisees and Sadducees. He then went to the area of Caesarea Philippi and, in verse 13, challenged the disciples with the famous question, "Who do people say that the Son of Man is?" The disciples gave some of the answers that they had heard being tossed about, but then Jesus got specific and personal in verse 15. "He said to them, 'But who do you say that I am?'"

Peter, not being someone who was shy about speaking up, answered with a statement that Jesus said was a revelation. "And Simon Peter answered and said, 'Thou are the Christ, the Son of the living God.'" Peter called Jesus the Christ—the Messiah—and this would carry with it all that we have talked about regarding the title of Messiah. He also referred to Jesus as the "Son of the living God." Just as a side note, we ought to mention that it is true that in the Old Testament, kings were referred to as sons of God, since they were seen as being established by God (2 Samuel 7:14; Psalm 2:7). The nation of Israel itself was referred to as God's son in Exodus 4:22. There may even be an allusion to the priests as sons of God in Malachi 1:6.

Jesus did not use this title for himself—although there is an indirect reference in the Parable of the Vine-growers in Mark 12, Matthew 21, and Luke 20—but the title was used by others for Jesus. We find Jesus being called *Son* by the voice from heaven at both Jesus's baptism and the transfiguration (Matthew 3:17; Mark 9:7). We see it used by Satan in Matthew 4:3 and by demons in Mark 5:7. Mark also tells us the centurion, at Jesus's crucifixion, proclaimed that Jesus was the Son of God.

All of the covenant/son images of Israel, kingship, and priesthood were fulfilled in Jesus. There were not to be many Messiahs, and the whole nation of Israel was not to be the Messiah. Paul understood this and called attention to it in Galatians 3:16, where he spoke about the Old Testament promises and, in particular, the covenant with Abraham: "Not the promises were spoken to Abraham and to his seed. He does not say, 'And to seeds,' as referring to many, but rather to one, 'And to your seed,' that is, Christ."

In using and accepting this name *Son*, Jesus was taking on the role of the fulfillment of Yahweh's promise to Abraham. He was allowing himself to be seen as the One who fulfills all of the prophecies and who is, in fact, the new Israel. However, the fact that there were others who were referred to as sons of God actually creates a problem. I knew a teacher for an adult Sunday School class who, one Advent Season, mentioned that there was something in the printed lesson that he had never heard before and he wondered if anyone else had noticed it. He had been a Sunday School teacher for many years in another denomination, and for several years in our church. He was a well-read high school teacher, so it came as a bit of a surprise when he finally said that what was new to him was the idea that Jesus *was* God—and not just the Son of God. Can one really be part of our churches for years and never hear about the divinity of Jesus?

We do use the word *son* figuratively in our regular language. It can mean an honorary position or an adopted position, and in that sense, we are all *sons of God*. Paul used this language in Galatians 4:5 when he said that Jesus was born into this world, "that He might redeem those who were under the Law, that we might receive the adoption as sons." But, while we might use *son* in this way, it most often means a much more direct connection and clearly implies a common essence.

As I have said often in trying to explain this, when a gorilla has a son, it is a gorilla. When a whale has a son it is a whale. When a human being has a son, it is a human being. When God has a Son, that Son is God. The difference is that it would be a different gorilla, whale, or human, because these are all finite beings. My use of the indefinite article "a" does get me into a bit of trouble here. Maybe Jesus is just "a" God, as the Jehovah's Witnesses say. It is true that while each *son* would carry the sense of *gorillaness,* or *whaleness,* or *humanness,* as finite creatures, each would be a different being than its parent. However, because God is an infinite being, there could be no division of being. The Son of God *is* God.

The mention of the indefinite article brings up another issue here. I have spent many hours over the years analyzing, and having discussions about, the indefinite article in John 1:1 but, even more to our point, discussing the meaning of "only begotten" (*monogenes*) in John 1:14. The claim is that Jesus was a created being. Jehovah created him first as the only being created by Jehovah, and then he created everything else. That fits the Jehovah's Witness doctrine that Jesus is "a God" lower than Jehovah but higher than the angels.

This argument is based on taking the Greek word *monogenes* apart to find its meaning. If you do take the words apart, you get the two parts *only* and *generated*—but words do not always work that way. If you take apart the word *wholesome,* you get two words dealing with quantity, but you would not find the word's true meaning, which is purity and healthfulness. A look at several Greek Lexicons tells us that the word *monogenes* means *unique* or *only* in the sense of being the only member of a particular kind. This is not a stretch of the language or forced interpretation (Thayer 1974, 417).

In Luke 7:12, the widow of Nain refers to her deceased son as her only son, and the word *monogenes* is used. The focus here is certainly not on his being her first *created*, child, but on his uniqueness: he was all she had. The same is true in Luke 8:42 and 9:38. These parents were asking for the healing of their only children because they were unique, and all they had. It was not merely because they had created them. This is especially clear in Hebrews 11:17, which speaks of Abraham offering up Isaac to God. Isaac was not Abraham's first-born nor his only son, but he was unique and special because he was chosen to carry on the covenant, and so Abraham refers to him as *monogenes*.

Before we move on, there is even more reason to see the language about Jesus as unique. Josh and Sean McDowell, in the updated edition of *Evidence That Demands A Verdict*, point this out:

> Some skeptics argue that Jesus' claims to sonship were not unique. Citing other biblical characters referred to as God's son, such as Adam, Moses, Solomon, or the nation of Israel, they question what makes Jesus' sonship exceptional. New Testament scholar Frank Thielman says the language used to describe Jesus' sonship is unique: "Mark uses the Greek adjective *agapetos* ('only beloved') in what Greek grammarians call the 'second attributive position.' An adjective in this position receives particular stress. In both [Mark] 1:11 and 9:7, therefore, God says that Jesus is 'my son—the uniquely beloved one" (Thielman, TNT, 63) (McDowell and McDowell 2017, 189).

The language makes it clear. Jesus is the Son of God, not in any created sense, not as a lesser God, but because of his unique relationship to God the Father. He is equal with the Father but has the relationship of Son as he obeys the Father. This is an act of his own will and stems from the love the Son has for the Father. As Jesus said in John 14:31, "that the world may know that I love the Father, and as the father gave Me commandment, even so I do." He had already shown that what He did, He did of his own will and authority—yet it is also out of love for the Father.

In this, we also see the love of the Father for the Son. "For this reason the Father loves Me, because I lay down my life that I may take it up again. No one has taken it away from me, but I lay it down on My own initiative. I have authority to lay it down, and I have authority to take it up again. This commandment I received from my Father" (John 10:17-18). The Son is not created, but is coeternal with the Father as one God. Their relationship within the one essence is a relationship of love between Father and Son.

This coeternal relationship would require the kind of Trinitarian nature of God we spoke of in chapter 1. We see this Trinitarian nature being displayed in Galatians, as we saw above, and when the author of Hebrews told us the promise God made to Abraham was all about Jesus. But we also see it in what are called Christophanies in the Old Testaments. These are places where an incarnate Yahweh appears. Since Yahweh is Spirit, and since the Scriptures say that no one has seen the Father, then theologians suggest that what we have here are pre-incarnate appearances of Jesus. One such place is in Genesis 18, where it is said the Yahweh appeared to Abraham. But in reading chapter 18, we see that it was three physical beings who approached Abraham. There was even an offer to wash their feet and an opportunity to share a meal with them.

As Abraham spent time with these three, he referred repeatedly to one of them as Yahweh. The second person of the Trinity is the incarnate one. Was this a pre-incarnation appearance of Jesus? The LORD then stays with Abraham as the two angels have their meeting with Lot. Following all of this is the destruction of Sodom and Gomorrah, where we are told, "Then the LORD rained on Sodom and Gomorrah brimstone and fire from the LORD out of heaven" (Genesis 19:22). It puzzles some people that there seems to be *two* Yahwehs in this verse, but what we are seeing is a clear statement about two persons of the Trinity, both of whom are Yahweh.

Charles Hodge clarifies the puzzle:

> With regard to this and similar remarkable expressions, the question is not, What may they mean? But, What do they mean? Taken by themselves they may be explained away, but taken in light of the connected revelations of God on the subject, it becomes apparent that Jehovah [Yahweh] is distinguished as a person from Jehovah [Yahweh]; and therefore that in the Godhead there is more than one person to whom the name Jehovah [Yahweh] belongs (Hodge 1997, 1:486).

Son of Man

Son of God is an important title for Jesus, but it is not the one he used most often for himself. Discussing the title of Son of God might raise in our minds the question about just what Jesus meant when he so often referred to himself as the "Son of Man." We might wonder, especially as we talk about the divinity of Jesus, why he so often used a phrase that seems to indicate just his humanity. Even though the explanation for this is well-known, we mention it here because the title appears at first glance to go against Jesus's other claims of deity.

It is true that this phrase can be used to refer to a human being. It is used this way in Psalm 8:4, where the psalmist was contemplating the glory of God, and the smallness of humanity in comparison to the greatness of the rest of creation, and so asked, "What is man that Thou dost take thought of him? And the son of man, that Thou dost take thought of him?"

Jesus used this phrase in a different way, one common to the Jewish literature of his day, and related to the Prophet Daniel. In the apocalyptic writings of the Jewish community, the Son of Man was seen as the one who will come at the end of time to judge us. This one will be pre-existing, bringing the power of God and having dominion over all the nations. Jesus identified himself with this Son of Man in places like Mark 14:62: "And Jesus said, 'I am, and you shall see the Son of Man sitting at the right hand of Power, and coming with the clouds of heaven." This use of the Son of Man title is directly connected to its usage in Daniel 7:13-14:

> I kept looking in the night visions,
> And behold, with the clouds of heaven
> One like a Son of Man was coming,
> And he came up to the Ancient of Days
> And was presented before Him.
> And to Him was given dominion,
> Glory and a kingdom,
> That all the peoples, nations, and men of every
> language
> Might serve Him.
> His dominion is an everlasting dominion
> Which will not pass away;
> And His kingdom is one
> Which will not be destroyed.

This is not the description of your average human being. To claim to be this Son of Man is to claim to be God. Lee Strobel quotes Craig Stromberg in reference to these verses:

"So look at what Jesus is doing by applying the term 'Son of Man' to himself," he continued. "This is someone who approaches God himself in his heavenly throne room and is given universal authority and dominion. That makes 'Son of Man' a title of great exaltation, not of mere humanity" (Strobel 1998, 30).

It is exactly this kind of power and imagery that Jesus attached to the term as we see in places like Matthew 24:30, "and then the sign of the Son of Man will appear in the sky, and then all the tribes of the earth will mourn, and they will see the Son of Man coming on the clouds of the sky with power and great glory." It is this title—with all of these attached images—which Jesus also applied to himself in places like Mark 8:38 and Luke 17:24. To use the phrase "the Son of Man" was clearly to claim divine power, but Jesus also used this title to show that he was the incarnate One who had come from the presence of the Father. In the discussion with Nicodemus where Jesus reminds us that all must be born again, and just before the well-known John 3:16, Jesus said to Nicodemus, "And no one has ascended into heaven, but He who descended from heaven, even the Son of Man" (John 3:13). Jesus claimed to be the Son of Man, come from heaven to be the Messiah and then return in victory. He did not hold back the need to share this truth.

In John 6, Jesus said some hard things about the eating of his flesh and the drinking of his blood. The people had a difficult time accepting his statements, especially since this was before the Last Supper. In essence, Jesus told them that if they thought these words were hard, "What then if you should behold the Son of Man ascending where He was before?" (John 6:62). Jesus said that they were going to see greater things than this following his death and resurrection and asked: How will you handle that?

So, yes the title *Son of God* does mean that Jesus was claiming to possess the nature of God, but *Son of Man* is not a claim to mere humanity, as Jesus used it in a specific context. Pulling the title Son of Man from the Old Testament, Jesus proclaimed his heavenly nature and also made clear that he was the connection between heaven and earth. He was the incarnation. He was the One who came to offer himself as a sacrifice and so needed to be fully human. He was the One who would cover sin committed against the holiness and righteousness of God, and only God could cover the sin committed against him. Jesus filled the role of *Son of Man*. He was the expression of the love of God appearing in our world, in our history. The attribute of God's love brought this Messiah, this son of Man, and Jesus made it clear he was the One. Other religious leaders were never so bold. Mohammed might have had a messiah complex. He might have wanted to do something for the Arab people of his day. But he did not claim to be God and Muslims would consider it the highest sin (*shirk*) if he had done so.

▼

CHAPTER FOUR

THE CLAIM TO BE JUDGE OF THE WORLD

"WHO ARE YOU to judge? Do you think you are God?" Common questions today any time someone even implies that there might be absolute truth or a moral standard.

It seems we naturally assume only God has the right to judge. One need not be perfect to make a judgment, but to be the ultimate judge of all things requires a different level of perfection. Before we look at Jesus's claim to be the judge of the world—a position of authority which, as we will note, requires a perfectly holy and omniscient Being (God/Yahweh)—we need to look at which attributes of God Jesus might be claiming for himself when he calls himself the judge of the world. At the top of the list of these attributes would be the holiness of God.

The Holiness of God

In the region of Western PA where I live, two well-known people have spoken to this issue in different ways. I live in Latrobe, the home of Mr. Rogers, who famously wrote a song about how even good people sometimes do bad things. There is always a failure in our goodness, no matter who we are and no matter our attempts to be good. But holiness means more than just being good. Latrobe is also just down the road from the Ligonier Valley, where Ligonier Ministries got its start. No one has spoken more about the topic of the holiness of God in the last generation than R. C. Sproul, and even though I am using my own notes to write this, I am sure my thoughts have been shaped by his thoughts.

But Dr. Sproul certainly did not invent this idea. The holiness of God has been a central notion in the discussion of God's attributes in all of church history. Hodge recognized its importance and power when he said, "Seraphim round about the throne who cry day and night, Holy, Holy, Holy is the Lord of hosts, give expression to the feelings of all unfallen rational creatures in view of the infinite purity of God. They are the representatives of the whole universe, in offering this perpetual homage to the divine holiness" (Hodge 1997, 1:413).

In approaching this topic, we will need to look at a number of Scriptures—but let's start with Isaiah 57:15:

> For thus says the high and exalted One
> Who lives forever, whose name is Holy,
> I dwell on a high and holy place,
> And also with the contrite and lowly of spirit
> In order to revive the spirit of the lowly
> And to revive the heart of the contrite.

Here we see a hint at what is meant by the term *holy*. The holiness of God is about God's transcendence: God's *set apartness*. This is what the Hebrew word *qadosh* means; a setting apart, a distinction. God is categorically different from us. God is above us and beyond us. Hosea 11:9 says,

> I will not execute My fierce anger;
> I will not destroy Ephraim again.
> For I am God and not man, the Holy One in your
> midst,
> And I will not come in wrath.

God is holy. God is awesome because we, while we can see God's image in us, are so unlike God that we stand in awe of such uncreated perfection. Some today do not like to use the word "awesome" when referring to God, since it has been so overused in our culture. After all, if a pair of shoes can be awesome, then the word has lost its meaning. But we see in the holiness of God a part of why God is the very definition of awesome. When we understand the transcendence and the *set apartness* of God, nothing else truly deserves to be called awesome.

We tend to think of holiness as primarily a moral or religious attitude. But the central idea of being holy is the idea of position or relationship between us and God. Obviously, we will see that holiness has a moral aspect. It does relate to the moral nature of God and the moral nature of those who trust in God. The prophet Habakkuk understood this when he said:

> Your eyes are too pure to approve evil,
> And You cannot look on wickedness with favor.
> Why do You look with favor
> On those who deal treacherously?
> Why are You silent when the wicked swallow up
> Those more righteous than they? (Habakkuk 1:13).

To be sure, God is holy in this moral sense, and that is why the prophet had to ask a question about the problem of evil. Many have asked, "If God is good, why is there evil?" But if God is not pure, holy, and righteous, then the question would not exist, and the problem of evil would fall apart. There would be no charge to bring against a good God for the evil in this world, since evil would also be part of God's nature.

So one of the things that the holiness of God means is that God is in no way influenced or tainted by the evil of the creation and also that the evil in this world is not a result of God's nature. It is important to see, however, that the ultimate focus on the attribute of holiness includes more than just moral rectitude. As God is categorically different than us, set apart from us, that is holy, then we become holy when we are set apart for God.

This is the foundation of how we share in holiness: by being set apart for God. Then the moral aspect comes as we live it out. This is why objects involved in worship, and even the entire Tabernacle and Temple, can be referred to as holy: they are set apart for the use of God. Even more so, this is what Peter was telling us in 1 Peter 1:14-16: "As obedient children, do not be conformed to the former lusts which were yours in your ignorance, but like the Holy One who called you, be holy yourselves also in all your behavior; because it is written, 'YOU SHALL BE HOLY, FOR I AM HOLY.'"

Holiness is our being set apart for God, and then it is displayed by our living as those who have been set apart. What we discover is that the more we understand the holiness of God, the more it changes our lives. It will even change our worship. "God, as He has no taint of sin in Himself, cannot tolerate it in the creature. The absolute holiness of God fences His love round; and without the constant recollection of it, worship degenerates either into pantheistic rapture, or impure mysticism" (Litton 1960, 71).

God is referred to as *holy* in nearly every book in the Old Testament. The Song of Moses in Exodus 15 states, in verse 11:

> Who is like You among the gods, O LORD?
> Who is like You, majestic in holiness,
> Awesome in praises, working wonders?

In Leviticus 19:2, we find the verse we saw quoted by Peter earlier connecting God's holiness to a call for us to be holy: "Speak to all the congregation of the sons of Israel and say to them, 'You shall be holy, for I the LORD your God am holy.'" Another example is in Psalm 99, where the psalmist is proclaiming the greatness of God and the ways in which God is distinct and transcendent above his creation. In this context, he writes in verse 3, "Let them praise Your great and awesome name; Holy is He" and then adds in verse 5: "Exalt the LORD our God And worship at His footstool; Holy is He."

Completing the praise to holiness, in verse 9 says:

> Exalt the LORD our God,
> And worship at His holy hill;
> For holy is the LORD our God.

This focus on the holiness of God becomes such a part of the faith that it becomes a title for God. Isaiah 1:4 calls God "The Holy One of Israel"—a title that is repeated twenty-four times in Isaiah alone.

We then come to the famous passage in Isaiah 6 where Isaiah has an amazing vision of the very throne of God. God is spoken of as *lofty* and *exalted*. God is surrounded by angelic beings who sing God's praises, "And one called out to another and said 'Holy, Holy, Holy, is the LORD of hosts, the whole earth is full of His glory.'" It is in the presence of the holy God that Isaiah now is confronted with a vastly different experience. He recognizes the distinction between Creator and creature. He understands his own moral imperfection.

The transcendence of holiness and the moral perfection of holiness overwhelm Isaiah. God then offers Isaiah forgiveness by fire, which displays for us the purification of the Holy Spirit. More than this, we must not miss that the fire comes from the altar, the place of shed blood, so it also tells us of the future work of Christ. In all of this, Isaiah receives forgiveness and goes on to do the work of a great prophet.

The threefold repetition of "Holy, Holy, Holy" in Isaiah's vision is seen again in the vision of God's throne in Revelation 4:8. Dr. Sproul says this formula, or *Trisagion* as it is called, is a way of expressing the centrality and ultimate importance of the holiness of God. He has said so in a number of lectures and explains when he writes,

> Only once in sacred Scripture is an attribute of God elevated to the third degree. Only once is a characteristic of God mentioned three times in succession. The Bible says that God is holy, holy, holy. Not that He is merely holy, or even holy, holy. He is holy, holy, holy, The Bible never says that God is love, love, love; or mercy, mercy, mercy; or wrath, wrath, wrath; or justice, justice, justice. It does say that He is holy, holy, holy, that the whole earth is full of his glory (Sproul 1998, 26).

Now we are not saying that holiness is a bigger or more powerful attribute than any of the others. We are also not saying that any of the attributes of God are incomplete and imperfect. But there is a focus here on holiness being a sort of binding attribute, a common theme in all of the attributes because this transcendence, the *set apartness* of God, tells us about God's very nature and the Creator/creature distinction that we keep coming back to.

We also do not want to see holiness as merely an Old Testament idea. We have seen Peter call us to holiness because God is holy, and we can see Paul calling us to live out our lives separate from the fallen world. Ephesians 5:27, a verse I've often used at weddings, reminds us of this call. We are told that Christ loved the church and gave himself as a sacrifice for a reason: "That he might present to Himself the church in all her glory, having no spot or wrinkle or any such thing; but that she should be holy and blameless."

In this passage, a Christian husband is told to act differently than the rest of the world because of his connection to the Holy Christ. All of this is based on the idea in verse 1 of imitating God. So be holy; be like God. Be holy as Christ is holy. Be separated. As the author of Hebrews described Jesus, "For it was fitting that we should have such a high priest, holy, innocent, undefiled, separated from sinners and exalted above the heavens" (Hebrews 7:27). As we will see, it is this status of Jesus—his holiness, his sinless life, his righteousness—which Jesus is presupposing when he claims that he will be the judge of the world.

One additional note on holiness is quite important. Holiness, both in the sense of transcendence and in the sense of moral rightness, is what defines the God of the Bible in comparison to the gods of other religions. The other gods of the Middle East, Egypt, Greece, Rome, and other pagan religions were not infinite. None of them were omnipresent, omniscient, or omnipotent. They were also themselves immoral. They lied, cheated, stole, and did pretty much anything evil that humans would do, only often on a bigger scale. They really were just larger, more powerful human beings. The gods of the East were infinite, but they were not personal. They were just the ultimate pantheistic oneness of the universe. This is why Francis Schaeffer liked to define the God of the Bible as "personal-infinite."

> The Bible says God is a living God and it tells us much about Him, but, most significantly perhaps, for twentieth-century man, it speaks of Him as both a personal God and an infinite God. This is the kind of God who is 'there', who exists. Furthermore, this is the only system, the only religion, that has this kind of God. The gods of the East are infinite by definition, in the sense that they encompass all—the evil as well as the good—but they are not personal. The gods of the West were personal, but they were very limited. The Teutonic, the Roman

and the Greek gods were all the same—personal
but not infinite. The Christian God, the God of
the Bible, is personal-infinite" (Schaeffer 1968, 25).

In the time that has passed since Francis Schaeffer wrote those
words, I have found it harder to speak of God as *personal* without
a bit of explanation. Many people think that when we say *personal*,
we mean he is our personal God; a God we personally possess or a
God in whatever form we prefer. But the word *personal* is not about
us; it is about God. What we mean is that God is a personal *being*;
God has personality. God thinks, acts, creates, loves, and has all
the attributes we think of when we think of personality. We have
personality because we are created in God's image. The pagan
Gods get their nature from human beings. The Christian God
shares his personal nature with us. We are called to be like him;
we do not expect him to act like us.

I have been asked, on occasion, how an infinite being can also
be personal. I am not sure I even see the problem here, but it seems
that the idea of a perfect and unbounded being is inconsistent with
what we think of as personal, which is usually something flawed
and finite. Field responded to this question in the context of God's
absolute being. The brackets are my words:

> It would be contradictory to speak of a round
> square, but there is no contradiction in speaking
> of a white, or a crimson square. So the adjectives
> personal and absolute [infinite] are not logical
> contradiction, nor are they contradictory in fact.
> When we speak of the absolute [infinite], we speak
> of it as a predicate of pure being, and what we mean
> is simply that the absolute is complete [unbounded]
> in itself, it has no conditions save conditions
> contained in itself. When we speak of personality
> we ascribe it to being, regarded as pure spiritual

being; and we simply mean that absolute personal being is, and must be, self-conscious, rational, and ethical; must answer to the idea of spirit. Why may not the Absolute [Infinite] Being be self-conscious? To deny this to Him would be to deny one of the perfections which even finite beings may have. Does the ascription of life, intelligence, personality to God militate in any degree against the dignity of the Infinite? (Field 1952, 25).

The Righteousness of God

In systematic theologies the attribute of God's righteousness is often discussed following the attribute of holiness. There is also often a connection made between holiness, righteousness, and judgment, since the understanding is that God's judgment will be fair and just, exactly because God is righteous. Ezra saw the righteousness of God in God's historic act of setting his people free, and he even sees it in relationship to our standing in judgment before a holy God. "O LORD God of Israel, Thou art righteous, for we have been left an escaped remnant, as it is this day, behold, we are before Thee in our guilt, for no one can stand before Thee because of this" (Ezra 9:15). The importance of this aspect of God's nature is driven home by the psalmist in Psalm 11:7:

> For the LORD is righteous; He loves righteousness;
> The upright will behold His face.

God loves righteousness. He will always do what is right and what is just. To do so is the very nature of God. We are not talking here about how we perceive God or how we experience the goodness of God. We are saying that God acts justly, righteously, in all of his thoughts and actions. This was Jesus's view of God the Father, and he shows it in John 17:25 when he calls God, "O righteous Father."

So it is God's nature to do justice; that is, to be righteous. God can do nothing else, as Abraham said in Genesis 18:25: "Shall not the Judge of the earth deal justly?" Again, we see justice and judgment connected. When Jesus claims to be the judge of the earth, he is claiming to be this righteous God. And it is because God is universally and consistently just that there can be a moral order in the creation.

I have always thought it to be a logical and rational question: If there is no moral, righteous, Creator, then how can there be a real moral ethic at all? It is a common protest from atheists who put forth the argument that they can be good without God, and that they are offended when believers say that atheists cannot be good people. First of all, I have never heard a Christian say that an atheist cannot be good without God. It would go against the clear teaching of Paul in the second chapter of Romans. My question, and I think the real question, is not whether an atheist can be a good person—but why would or should they? On what basis, and for what reason, would an atheist be good, or even be able to distinguish between good and evil?

Some people balk at God setting standards for his creation, saying that God acted arbitrarily in setting standards and moral laws. The implication is that God acted just because he did not want us to have any fun. But righteousness has to do with keeping the law and doing the right thing. There is no law above God and so, as an attribute of God, righteousness refers to the consistency of God's own nature and the perfection of God living according to that nature in both personality and essence. In the area of Christian ethics a couple of questions confront the believer. Are God's laws arbitrary? Is something wrong because God said so, or did God say so because it is wrong? We have an answer. All that God does is according to the very nature of God. God is truth, so it is wrong to lie. God is faithful, so adultery is wrong. God is the author of life, so murder is wrong. It all comes from God's nature.

This means that things are right or wrong because God says so—but he says so according to his very nature, not arbitrarily, and not on the basis of some law above God. It helps to notice here that there are several words translated as righteousness in the Bible. They all carry more than just the idea of doing right, though that is part of all the definitions. They also include the idea of being in good standing as part of a community. Righteousness takes on, then, the sense of justice. Righteousness and justice cannot be separated. This forms the basis for what Paul tells us in Romans 3:21-26 as he defends God's righteousness:

> But now apart from the Law the righteousness of God has been manifested, being witnessed by the Law and the Prophets, even the righteousness of God through faith in Jesus Christ for all those who believe; for there is no distinction; for all have sinned and fall short of the glory of God, being justified as a gift by His grace through the redemption which is in Christ Jesus; who God displayed publicly as a propitiation in His blood through faith. This was to demonstrate His righteousness, because in the forbearance of God He passed over the sins previously committed; for the demonstration, I say, of His righteousness at the present time, that He might be just and the justifier of the one who has faith in Jesus.

Paul tells us that God is right and he is just, even when it does not look that way. God has kept the covenant he made with Abraham and has now acted in history to deal with sin and evil. God can act with righteous justice and still offer forgiveness because God has appeased his own goodness and perfection in the sacrifice of his Son. So God can retain his justice, even as he offers justification and redemption to us, and this in itself displays his righteousness.

What an amazing thing it is! The righteousness of God is demonstrated in the saving act of Jesus as he sacrificed for us, and it will be the righteousness of God that is acting in Jesus when he acts as judge of all the earth. But before we look at the claim of Jesus, let's look briefly at two other attributes of God that come into play as Jesus claims to be judge of all the earth.

The Perfection of God

We talked in chapter 2 about the self-existence of God. No one created God. God has always been, because God has the power to be, to exist, as part of his very nature. Following from God's self-existence we see that God is unchanging. There are two aspects to this unchanging nature that are sometimes seen as two attributes and sometimes as two ways of speaking about God's unchanging nature. We will look at perfection first and then simplicity.

We can see in Psalm 102:24-27 the underlying assumption in the Old Testament that God is unchanging. We also see that this idea brings comfort:

> I say, "O my God, do not take me away in the midst
> of my days,
> Your years are throughout all generations.
> "Of old You founded the earth,
> And the heavens are the work of Your hands.
> "Even they will perish, but You endure;
> And all of them will wear out like a garment;
> Like clothing You will change them and they will
> be changed.
> "But You are the same,
> And Your years will not come to an end.

In Deuteronomy 32:4, Moses tells us that Yahweh is,

> The Rock! His work is perfect,
> For all His ways are just;
> A God of faithfulness and without injustice,
> Righteous and upright is He.

Again in the Psalms we are told:

> The law of the LORD is perfect, restoring the soul,
> The testimony of the LORD is sure, making wise
> the simple (Psalm 19:7).

Jesus affirmed the perfection of God in the Sermon on the Mount when, in Matthew 5:48, he said, "Therefore you are to be perfect, as your heavenly Father is perfect." The word "perfect" here is the translation of *teleioi* and *teleios*, which speak of reaching a desired purpose. We are to become what God desires us to become, to reach the fullness of what God intends for us as his covenant people. As finite beings, we will not reach God's level of infinite, unchanging perfection. So it is a comfort to know that God can be counted upon even if we cannot. His nature is unchanging.

Because God is perfect, what would there be to change? Change to what? God is perfection. In God's being, purpose, and promises, God is perfect. This does not mean that God is static or inactive. It means there is no change in God's being or in his nature. God is always active, but you can trust God to have the same nature—that is, to be the same God. God is not capricious or moody. His consistency is a comfort to us. One who is consistent is one who can be trusted.

When people say that God created right and wrong arbitrarily, we can point out that the God revealed in the Bible is not arbitrary. God's actions are always consistent with his nature, and the laws of God given to us are there because they are consistent with his nature. For Christians, this has always included the understanding that God is unchanging in his knowledge and therefore is omniscient. We will talk more about that in chapter 6.

Does this mean that God must always treat people the same or respond to every situation exactly the same? In Malachi 3:6, God says, "For I the LORD, do not change; therefore you, O sons of Jacob, are not consumed." God had consumed, or judged, others for their sin. Why not the sons of Jacob? The rebellion of Edom was condemned just a couple of chapters earlier, and now the sons of Jacob are off the hook. But these were different circumstances.

What we are claiming here is that God is consistent within himself. How God's consistent nature works itself out in your life might be different than how it works itself out in another's life. We understand how a parent's yes to one child and a no to another can both be based on their love for each child in his or her own circumstances. God might heal one person and not another, and both actions might be based on the same consistent love of God.

Some point out that the Bible speaks at times of God changing his mind or even repenting of what he has done. This is, first of all, anthropomorphic language. It relates to the way we experience God's actions, and not to any change in the nature of God. If I promise you that I will buy you an ice cream cone if you follow me to Dairy Queen, and then you do not follow me to Dairy Queen, my not buying you ice cream means I am being perfectly consistent. One way you get the ice cream, the other way you do not, and yet there would be no change in me. I might be unhappy that you do not get the ice cream, but if I am a consistent person, that is what will happen. Likewise, just because God cannot change, it does not mean that God does not feel a response when humans get things wrong. God is also personal.

What we are saying is that many of God's promises are contingent. "If you do such and such, then I will bless you." If we do not keep the "if," God does not keep the "then." It might seem to us who were counting on that promise that God has changed. In fact, God has been perfectly consistent. As we talk of God's unchanging and perfect nature, sometimes I think the best word for our understanding is *consistency*. God is consistent. He is not frozen but is always morally consistent with his own nature.

The Simplicity of God

The unchanging nature of God also means there is a simplicity to God. By this we mean that God is totally integrated. It is what we meant earlier when we said that all of these various attributes of God are not parts that, when added together, form God. All of these attributes are unified in one God with one nature. Every aspect of God is related to, and integrated with, all other aspects. God is perfect harmony. We know that there is only one God. Deuteronomy 6:4 tells us, "Hear, O Israel! The LORD is our God, the LORD is one!" and James 2:19 says, "You believe that God is one. You do well; the demons also believe, and shudder." These verses make this clear.

Then, because of the perfect, unchangeable nature of God, we see also a simplicity in this one God:

> God's oneness includes more than his numerical unity. It comprises also his simplicity. This becomes clear when one considers the fact that the Scripture in giving us a description of the fullness of God's being uses not only adjectives but also nouns: it tells us not only that God is faithful, righteous, living, omniscient, loving, wise etc., but also that he is the truth, righteousness, life, light, love, wisdom, etc. Jer. 10:10; 23:6; John 1:4, 5, 9; 14:16; I Cor. 1:30; I John 1:5; 4:8; and that every attribute is identical with God's being by reason of the fact that every one of his virtues is absolutely perfect (Bavinck 1985, 168).

Now as we move on to the claims of Jesus, we see that it is the holiness and righteousness of God that sets the stage for judgment. These attributes involve the whole nature of God and are in perfect union within God's nature. Only a God with such attributes would have the right to act as judge of the world, and that is exactly what Jesus claims for himself.

Jesus Claimed to be Judge of the World

The holiness and righteousness of God—as well as omniscience, justice, mercy, and love—enable God to be the perfect and absolute judge of the creation. We are looking to see if Jesus makes the claim to be that God. We are trying to make the connection between Yahweh and Jesus, to show that they are the same being, according to Jesus's own claims

In John 5:22-23, the enemies of Jesus were looking to kill him. They were upset because they claimed that Jesus "was calling God His own Father, making Himself equal with God" (John 5:18). Even if people in our day, two millennia later, think Jesus did not claim to be God, it sure seems that those who were in his presence then thought he was making that exact claim. Jesus's response to this threat was to speak of the relationship between the Son and the Father. He claimed that the same honor given to the Father should be given to the Son, since the Son is the judge of all people.

In John 5:22-23, Jesus said, "For not even the Father judges anyone, but He has given all judgment to the Son, so that all will honor the Son even as they honor the Father. He who does not honor the Son does not honor the Father who sent Him." This was shocking to the hearers, who were aware that the Hebrew Scripture taught that they were to worship Yahweh, at least in part, because he was the judge of the world.

Psalm 96 is a call to worship on the basis of the righteous judgment of Yahweh. Verses 7-13 show us that call:

> Ascribe to the LORD, O families of the peoples,
> Ascribe to the LORD glory and strength.
> Ascribe to the LORD the glory of His name;
> Bring an offering and come into His courts.
> Worship the LORD in holy attire;
> Tremble before Him, all the earth.
> Say among the nations, "The LORD reigns;

> Indeed, the world is firmly established, it will not
> be moved;
> He will judge the peoples with equity."
> Let the heavens be glad, and let the earth rejoice;
> Let the sea roar, and all it contains;
> Let the field exult, and all that is in it.
> Then all the trees of the forest will sing for joy
> Before the LORD, for He is coming,
> For He is coming to judge the earth.
> He will judge the world in righteousness,
> And the peoples in His faithfulness.

We might not normally think that considering God as judge would bring us to worship, but maybe we need to rethink that view. The celebration here is the joy of a God who will judge in total righteousness, holiness, and in the context of grace and love.

The same concept is shown in a couple of more contemporary examples. The psalmist is looking forward to "the end of days," to use the words of British author J.R.R. Tolkien (Tolkien 1977, 13). Tolkien wrote a number of times of what will happen at the end of the history of Middle Earth, which included a setting right of all things. We see the same imagery in the last book of the Narnia Series by another British author, C.S. Lewis; before the end of the world, all come to Aslan's Country and all things are set right (Lewis 1976).

In the process of judgment, we might experience wrath, from our perspective—but the judgment itself is, in actuality, a good and righteous event. The judgment means God will be setting all evil right. In Psalm 96, the writer was clear about this, and we see just a couple of Psalms later the same connection between worship and the judgment of Yahweh. Psalm 98:4-9 brings us to joyful worship, and yet is based on the righteous judgment of God:

> Shout joyfully to the LORD, all the earth;
> Break forth and sing for joy and sing praises.
> Sing praises to the LORD with the lyre,
> With the lyre and the sound of melody.
> With trumpets and the sound of the horn
> Shout joyfully before the King, the LORD.
> Let the sea roar and all it contains,
> The world and those who dwell in it.
> Let the rivers clap their hands,
> Let the mountains sing together for joy
> Before the LORD, for He is coming to judge the
> earth;
> He will judge the world with righteousness
> And the peoples with equity.

These Scriptures tell us to worship God, at least in part, because he is judge. Jesus claimed that he should receive the same honor and worship when he claimed to be the judge spoken of in the Old Testament.

We have seen how Jesus uses the title "Son of Man" for himself. In Matthew 25:31-34, he uses that title to describe himself as judge of all people:

> But when the Son of Man comes in His glory, and
> all the angels with Him, then He will sit on His
> glorious throne. All the nations will be gathered
> before Him; and He will separate them from one
> another, as the shepherd separates the sheep from
> the goats; and He will put the sheep on His right,
> and the goats on the left. Then the King will say to
> those on His right, 'Come, you who are blessed of
> My Father, inherit the kingdom prepared for you
> from the foundation of the world.

In the rest of Matthew 25, Jesus explained how his judgment would be worked out. He couched this teaching in parables about judgment and then applied them to his own coming acts as judge, when *he* will be the one to separate the sheep from the goats. These parables clearly show that the master has a right to handle his own property as he sees fit and to reward his people according to his relationship with them and their trust in him.

In these parables, and in Jesus's teaching in Matthew 25:31-34, Jesus claimed to be this Master. In John 5, just after the passage we looked at earlier, Jesus made the same reference to the Son of Man being the judge. In verses 26 and 27, Jesus said, "For just as the Father has life in Himself, even so He gave to the Son also to have life in Himself, and He gave Him authority to execute judgment, because He is the Son of Man."

This teaching by Jesus also takes us directly back to the prophet Ezekiel, who spoke in chapter 14 about the judgment of God when God will come to gather his sheep and separate the sheep from the goats. We might miss this direct reference to Ezekiel by Jesus—the clear claim he made to be the God of Israel who brings this judgment spoken of by Ezekiel—but the people of his day did not miss it.

In this section of Matthew, as well as in Luke 19, Jesus told parables that expanded his claim to be the judge of the world. In each of these passages, Jesus was clear about what he was getting at in these parables, and he told them as illustrations of his clear claim that the Son of Man would judge the world.

In John 9:39, we see that Jesus had just healed a man born blind. Jesus and the Pharisees were at odds over this event. I am always amazed that the Pharisees had before them a man claiming to have been born blind who was now healed, but all they could think about was that this healing took place on the Sabbath. They apparently had no amazement at the miracle. Talk about majoring on the minors.

The Pharisees interviewed the man and then dismissed him,

not too impressed with his answers. Jesus then found the formerly blind man and presented himself, and challenged the man to faith. In that discussion, Jesus said, "For judgment I came into this world, so that those who do not see may see, and that those who see may become blind." Clearly, the judgment we have been speaking of has been about what will happen when Jesus returns and acts as judge for the world. Here, however, he is pointing out that his very presence and teaching bring a sort of judgment in preparation for the final judgment. It is that he, Jesus, sets the standard by his very presence. While he might not act as judge during his first coming, his very holiness and divinity sets a standard by which all things are judged. In that sense, judgment follows him and has already started.

This is what Jesus was getting at in John 3:17 when he made a statement that seems to run counter to our claim in this chapter. "For God did not send the Son into the world to judge the world; but that the world should be saved through Him." So, did Jesus come as judge or not? As we saw in John 10, Jesus makes a connection between the final judgment and his presence on earth as savior. Judgment has already begun because of his presence in this world. The standard is set: those who believe will not be judged as to where they will spend eternity. They will be with God. Those who do not believe have been judged already, for they will spend eternity apart from God. There is judgment because the light has come into the world; the standard has been set. The final act of judgment will come at the end of days, but the standard has already been set by Jesus's presence.

Jesus revealed another interesting detail about the judgment and his authority when, in John 12:48, he said, "He who rejects Me and does not receive My sayings, has one who judges him; the word I spoke is what will judge him at the last day." The very words, the truth, of Jesus will be the standard of judgment, just as we saw in John 3 and 10. Yet, we see again that such statements can only be made in reference to the God of the Old Testament. In I Samuel 2, we see Hannah's Song, a poem that sets the pattern for what Mary offers up as praise in the Magnificat in Luke 1.

1 Samuel 2:10 tells us it is Yahweh who will be the judge of the whole earth:

> Those who contend with the LORD will be shattered;
> Against them He will thunder in the heavens,
> The LORD will judge the ends of the earth;
> And He will give strength to His king,
> And will exalt the horn of His anointed.

The judgment is God's prerogative and even though, from our perspective, it may come to us as wrath, it is the just action of a holy God. Such judgment is not at odds with God's love, mercy, or grace. It is based upon these attributes because God, in his simplicity, is in complete balance.

This is not to underplay how we see the judgment day of God described. Isaiah 66:15-16 describes the judgment in a prophet's voice:

> For behold, the LORD will come in fire
> And His chariots like the whirlwind,
> To render His anger with fury,
> And His rebuke with flames of fire.
> For the LORD will execute judgment by fire
> And by His sword on all flesh,
> And those slain by the LORD will be many.

When what is unholy stands before Holiness, the consequences might not be a pretty sight, but they will be good and just. This day of judgement belongs to the LORD: I use all capitals here, since the word is *Yahweh*. In the chapter made famous by Pete Seeger's song "Turn, Turn, Turn," the author of Ecclesiastes goes on to say, "I said to myself, 'God will judge both the righteous man and the wicked man,' for a time for every matter and for every deed is there" (Ecclesiastes 3:17).

The Apostolic Witness

The day of judgement became known as "The Day of Yahweh." Joel describes the judgment, once again with the power of a prophet, and in 3:14 speaks of this day as "The day of the LORD." Zephaniah 1:7 and 14 both speak of the "day of the LORD." Isaiah speaks out against Babylon in chapter 13 and says in verse 6: "Wail, for the day of the LORD is near! It will come as destruction from the almighty."

What is amazing is that we have in the New Testament faithful Jewish men writing about that day that is to come and referring to it as a day that will reveal the authority of Jesus. If the Day of Yahweh is also seen as the Day of Jesus, then Jesus is seen as the equal of Yahweh.

Paul makes this connection in several places. In Philippians 1:6, we have one of the great promises of hope. "For I am confident of this very thing, that He who began a good work in you will perfect it until the day of Christ Jesus." The day of Yahweh, on which he will judge, has now become the day of Christ Jesus. Then, in the next chapter, we see Paul calling on believers to live so as to show their faith in the middle of a broken and evil world. They should do this by "holding fast the word of life, so that in the day of Christ I may have cause to glory because I did not run in vain nor toil in vain" (Philippians 2:16).

Paul also speaks in this way in 2 Corinthians 1:14, but with slightly different language. Paul told the Corinthians that what he was writing to them was consistent with what had already been said, and that he hoped they would remember his teaching until the end, "just as you also partially did understand us, that we are your reason to be proud as you also are ours, in the day of our Lord

Jesus." Paul certainly knew the Hebrew Bible. He might have been one of the best Bible scholars of his day. He knew the prophets had spoken of the judgment day as the day of Yahweh, so to change that language was to reveal a dramatic claim concerning the nature of Jesus.

Paul was not the only one to proclaim Jesus as judge of all the earth. Peter proclaimed the same message in his sermon in Acts 10. He also made it clear that what was being said about Jesus came from Jesus's own teaching. "And He ordered us to preach to the people. And solemnly testify that this is the One who has been appointed by God as Judge of the living and the dead" (Acts 10:42).

We might be talking about the apostolic witness, but it is clear that they see their witness to Jesus as judge as coming from the teachings of Jesus himself. As we look at Acts, we should notice that here, too, Paul speaks of Jesus as judge and connects the authority for that judgment to the resurrection of Christ. In Acts 17:30-31, in Paul's message to the people of Athens at the Areopagus, he makes the connection between repentance, resurrection, and the authority of Christ as judge: "Therefore having overlooked the times of ignorance, God is now declaring to men that all people everywhere should repent, because He has fixed a day in which He will judge the world in righteousness through a Man whom He has appointed, having furnished proof to all men by raising Him from the dead."

Along with all of this, we need to be aware of how Isaiah 66 is seen as fulfilled in Jesus. Remember, the words of Isaiah 66 begin with God coming in fury and flame and then focus on the words of Paul in II Thess. 1:5-10 as he speaks of the coming of Jesus in judgment:

> This is a plain indication of God's righteous judgment so that you will be considered worthy of the kingdom of God, for which indeed you are suffering. For after all it is only just for God to

repay with affliction those who afflict you, and to give relief to you who are afflicted and to us as well when the Lord Jesus will be revealed from heaven with His mighty angels in flaming fire, dealing out retribution to those who do not know God and to those who do not obey the gospel of our Lord Jesus. These will pay the penalty of eternal destruction, away from the presence of the Lord and from the glory of His power, when He comes to be glorified in His saints on that day, and to be marveled at among all who have believed, for our testimony to you was believed.

The image of the day of Yahweh from Isaiah 66 is now applied to Jesus when he returns. And all of this is not just found in Peter and Paul. We see in Revelation that John gives an even more dramatic picture of Jesus coming in power. In Revelation 19, we see the marriage supper of the Lamb describing the great fellowship of believers in the presence of Jesus and then the coming of Jesus to earth to judge and to rule. Again, we see the imagery of Isaiah now applied to Jesus in verses 11-16:

And I saw heaven opened, and behold, a white horse, and He who sat on it is called Faithful and True, and in righteousness He judges and wages war. His eyes are a flame of fire, and on His head are many diadems; and He has a name written on Him which no one knows except Himself. He is clothed with a robe dipped in blood, and His name is called The Word of God. And the armies which are in heaven, clothed in fine linen, white and clean, were following Him on white horses. From His mouth comes a sharp sword, so that with it He may strike down the nations, and He will rule

> them with a rod of iron; and He treads the wine
> press of the fierce wrath of God, the Almighty.
> And on His robe and on His thigh He has a name
> written, "KING OF KINGS, AND LORD OF
> LORDS."

Because of who Jesus is, and because he has come to offer salvation, this understanding is not a source of fear for the believer. We trust in God's justice, holiness, and righteousness and, with Jesus as the One who saves, we may approach that day with confidence as well as reverence. As American Christian singer-songwriter Michael Card sings, we will look into the face of our judge and see a savior there (Card 1989).

Jesus is the savior, but it is also before his judgment seat that we will stand (2 Corinthians 5:10). This paradox is profound. Paul goes on, in the same chapter in Corinthians, to say that this Jesus before whom we stand in judgment is also the one through whom God is "reconciling the world to Himself, not counting their trespasses against them" (2 Corinthians 5:19).

Jesus claims to be the judge of the world. That claim can only be made by God. His apostles agreed that he was worthy of that title and position. What was there about Jesus that connected him, in the minds of the apostles, with the Holy One of Israel, who alone has the right to make this final judgment?

The Sinlessness of Jesus

As we have noted, any time we make any kind of moral or ethical statement in our culture, there is always someone who responds, "Who are *you* to judge?" That is usually a frustrating question, because most often, we are not judging at all. We are submitting that there is a higher authority than us who does have a right to judge and who has spoken on the issue at hand. The question is also based on a *you too* fallacy that says: You cannot say I am guilty because *you too* are guilty.

It might be a fallacy logically, but it feels convincing emotionally. We think (feel?) that someone should be better than us if they are going to judge us. In that case, a judge of all would need to be perfect and without fault. Jesus took on the right to judge because he is God and then amazingly displayed his right to judge by living a sinless life of obedience to God the Father. In this way, Jesus was completely set apart from all other human beings. He demonstrated a morally perfect life, with the holiness of God visible in every area.

It has been pointed out many times that no other religious leader or founder could ask the question Jesus asked in John 8:46: "Which one of you convicts Me of sin?" All of us can claim great skills and abilities, but none can claim moral perfection: to be without sin. And yet Jesus backed this claim up. We know this because others saw it in him. Pilate said to the chief priests, "I find no guilt in this man" (Luke 23:4). The thief on the cross said that Jesus had done nothing wrong. In response to the mocking of the other criminal hanging with them, his reply was that they were under condemnation, "And we indeed justly, for we are receiving what we deserve for our deeds; but this man has done nothing wrong" (Luke 23:41).

Now, these two examples might have been meant in a limited way. Some might say they do not necessarily mean sinless perfection. But they are not the end of the testimony. In fact, those who knew Jesus far better than Pilate or the thief on the cross spoke more clearly of his sinlessness. Peter said that we are redeemed with precious blood as he recalls the Old Covenant sacrificial system, and then applies it to Jesus, whose blood was, "as of a lamb unblemished and spotless, the blood of Christ" (1 Peter 1:19). Peter then quotes Isaiah and applies the prophecy of the coming suffering servant to Jesus, "who committed no sin, nor was any deceit found in His mouth" (1 Peter. 2:22).

John, who might have known Jesus better than anyone, also made this claim concerning him: "My little children, I am writing these things to you so that you may not sin. And if anyone sins, we have an Advocate with the Father, Jesus Christ the righteous" (1 John 2:1). Then again in 1 John 3:7, he writes, "Little children, make sure no one deceives you; the one who practices righteousness is righteous, just as He is righteous." Jesus is the righteous One, completely without sin and completely obedient to the Father—in contrast to our first representative, Adam.

Some hesitate at the notion of Jesus being obedient, because it sounds as if Jesus is inferior to the Father. But if there is one God, and Jesus and the father are of the same essence, then they are always in complete agreement. Obedience in the incarnation displays the worth of the incarnate Jesus to be our sacrifice and to be the judge of sin. This is what Paul was talking about in 2 Corinthians 5:21: "He made Him who knew no sin to be sin on our behalf, so that we might become the righteousness of God in Him." Jesus knew no sin, and yet he took its consequences on himself for us, so that we might become righteous and that we might display the righteousness of God.

Now it was not that Jesus, in the context of the incarnation, was not tempted to sin. What is central is that he did not give in to the temptation. The book of Hebrews tells us that Jesus was "without sin" (4:15), "undefiled" (7:26), and "without blemish" (9:14). Some people wonder about this. If Jesus did not sin, was he fully human? That is a fair question, but let's look at the Hebrews 4:15 verse we just noted: "For we do not have a high priest who cannot sympathize with our weaknesses, but One who has been tempted in all things as we are, yet without sin."

Were not Adam and Eve human before they sinned? Sin is now our normal state, since the fall, but it is not a necessary component of humanity. It is not how God created us. This is the fatal flaw in the argument that there could not be an intelligent designer since there are so many problems in the creation, such as genetic disease. But what we see is a fallen, broken creation. We, as humans, brought evil into the world.

More to the point of Jesus's temptation: I have noticed many times, while in the midst of trying to lose a pound or two, that temptation gets stronger when you do not give into it. No sweets today, no problem. Second day, a little harder, and the third day, much worse. By the second week, I am thinking, "Where are the M&Ms?" So Jesus took on a burden that was greater than all of ours. He avoided all sin and dealt with its increasing temptation, yet he remained obedient to the Father and did not sin. You do not know the full power of temptation by giving into it: you experience its power by *not* giving in. Jesus never gave in. He did what Adam could not do, and therefore his sacrifice was a perfect sacrifice and of divine worth.

The sinlessness of Jesus validates his claim to be worthy to judge the world. The only judge of the world is Yahweh. Jesus is Yahweh, come to be among us. His perfection reminds us of our imperfection, but it also means we have a savior, a perfect representative who has taken our place. The baby in a manger grew up and never lost his sinless nature, and yet took the punishment for our sin. That truth, when you believe it and live it by faith, will set you free.

CHAPTER FIVE

▼

THE CLAIM TO LORDSHIP

JESUS CLAIMED TO be God by claiming specific attributes and titles. The attribute of God we want to explore in this chapter is God's omnipotence and the closely associated notion of God's sovereignty and Lordship over his creation. Then we will see how, when Jesus claimed to have mastery over the creation, to be Lord of the Sabbath, and to have the authority to send both the angels and the Holy Spirit, he was claiming omnipotence—and therefore deity.

One of the names or titles given to God in the Old Testament is *El Shaddai*, which is often translated *The Almighty*. This is one of the oldest names for God in Scripture and is the most frequently used title for God. It might have been the highest name for God until the revealing of the name YHWH to Moses. God even affirmed this in Exodus 6:2, when God told Moses that he had revealed himself to Abraham, Isaac, and Jacob as El Shaddai, but that he had not made himself know to them by his name; Yahweh.

Now, even though we often translate this name as *The Almighty,* it literally can mean *the sufficient one* or *the thunderer* or *the overpowerer.* It has to do with sufficient strength and power. There is an event in Numbers chapter 11 that I always liked to tell at Vacation Bible School and youth groups. The people of Israel were on the Exodus, and in the middle of the wilderness they became grumpy. They were thrilled when God first sent them manna to eat, but they got pretty tired of it after a while. As I heard an old missionary say one time, they had baked manna, ground manna, boiled manna, manna cakes, all sorts of manna concoctions. They were so desperate that they looked back on Egypt as a good place, because at least there they had "the cucumbers, and the melons and the leeks and the onion and the garlic" (Numbers 11:5). They were actually whining about leeks! (No offence to leek lovers.) What they really wanted was meat.

Moses complained to God that this was a bigger mess than he could handle. He wanted to know just how he was supposed to feed all of these people. He even looked to God and said, in effect, "I didn't bring them to this place, so why should I carry this burden? God, you take care of it." Then, getting more dramatic, he suggested that if God was going to leave him in charge of this multitude of complainers, then God should just take his life now.

God responded to this ingratitude by proclaiming that he would give them meat every day for a month, until it came out their nostrils. And some say God does not have a sense of humor! Moses wondered where God would get all of this meat. God responded with a question: "Is the LORD'S power limited?" (Numbers 11:23). Then the rest of the chapter goes on to display that God is sufficient, all powerful, and able to do everything that he desires. His power is not limited. He is El Shaddai.

The name El Shaddai tells us that God is the sufficient cause for all things. It is the way God introduced himself to Abraham (Genesis 17:1). It is the nature of God so often spoken of in the Old Testament, when it refers to the right hand of God. The attribute of God we are talking about here is omnipotence. Omnipotence is the infinity of God expressed in the terms of the power of God. In

Job 42:2, Job says to God: "I know that Thou canst do all things, And that no purpose of Thine can be thwarted." So omnipotence means not only that God has unlimited power, but that God, as a personal being, has a purpose for his actions and there is nothing in existence that can stop God from carrying out his plan. Psalm 115:3 says, "But our God is in the heavens; He does whatever He pleases."

For humans, our power is really just the use of our will to direct the power found outside of us. We do not have power as a part of our nature. It is added on to us. I have been amused in pastoring some small churches that have power struggles, even when there really was not that much power to struggle over. We, as finite creatures, always seem to seek power. God's power is inherent within God. God does not use his will to gain power, because power is a part of the makeup of his will. His power is always creative; it does not build on power from anything beyond God, it creates all that is beyond God. As always, this seemingly abstract doctrine is practical when we look at it more closely. We will come back to the notion of sovereignty in a moment, but notice first the practical implications of what it means that God governs in a sovereign way all created realities, including you.

> Whatever the LORD pleases, He does,
> In heaven and in earth, in the seas and all deeps
> (Psalm 135:6).

This means that, because God is infinite and omnipotent, and because God has no boundaries, he is able to care for you and know you as if no one else in the world existed. Your little problems and minor prayers are not a nuisance to God. You are not bothering God, or taking up his limited resources. God does not have *bigger things* to worry about. An infinite, omnipotent God can handle all of it. His nature is power, omnipotent power, and love combined.

God is free to do, and able to do, all things according to his nature. *According to his nature* is an important phrase. God cannot do the logically absurd or what is contradictory. God cannot change the past. God cannot lie. God cannot break his promises or be evil or cruel. It is not because there is some outside standard or force preventing God from these things, but because God's nature will not allow such things.

People sometimes ask questions to mock God. Can God make a square circle? Can God make a rock so big even he can't move it? The implication is that if God can't do these things, God isn't all powerful. But someone's ability to put contradictory words together is not a limitation on God—it is a display of their own inconsistency. In other words, God is too smart to be caught in our finite contradictions. Just because you can put together a contradictory statement does not mean that God is required to act on your irrational thoughts. As St. Ambrose said, "What is impossible to God? Not that which is difficult to His power, but that which is contrary to His nature" (Castle 1983, 172).

The omnipotence of God is displayed in the creation by his sovereignty. God is free to do, and able to do, all things according to God's nature. There is no aspect or part of creation over which God is not sovereign. Now, some immediately think this means some kind of determinism. It is true that God's will always comes to pass, and that all things that do come to pass are ultimately his will. Still sounds like determinism? Let's look a little closer.

God is, first of all, sovereign in his will. God is said to have a *decretive* will, which is that aspect of God's omnipotent will by which God decrees what shall come to pass. This will of God is always accomplished. God also has what some call his *permissive* will. This will is displayed in the rules and guidelines of life that God has given to us as free creatures. This will can be disobeyed. It is God's will, for instance, that we do not murder—yet this has often been disobeyed. God has given us many such commands, and notice this: all of them are consistent with his nature.

God is totally free in the acts of his will. His acts are not arbitrary or indifferent. God has reasons from within his own nature, and there is nothing outside of God that can influence his will. We see the comments of Jesus in Matthew 19:26: "And looking at them Jesus said to them, 'With people this is impossible, but with God all things are possible'" and in Mark 14:36: "And He was saying, 'Abba! Father! All things are possible for You; remove this cup from Me; yet not what I will, but what You will.'" Jesus is not implying that God would ever do anything outside of his own nature. There are things God would never do, and ways God would never act—but this is no limit to his power. Instead, it is an affirmation that there is no power beyond God.

In my ethics class, we talk about what it takes to live ethically. First, there is knowledge—because truth precedes compassion. This is an idea I have been emphasizing for years. You have to know what is right before you can do the right thing. In our culture these days, and even in the organized church, many people are confused about where the truth comes from. Second, there is the will. You must have the will to do what you know is right. Third, you must have the ability to accomplish what you know is right. God certainly has all three of these in an unlimited degree, and so God's actions are always ethical.

We come then to the understanding that God is not only sovereign in his will, but also in his power. This is omnipotence in terms of God's rule of the universe, but it is important to note that, in God's sovereignty, God has established and chosen to work through secondary causes. For this reason, the Biblical view is *not* determinism. God has chosen to work through our freedom.

> Nor is omnipotence inconsistent with God's acting, sometimes independently of secondary causes (as in creation), and sometimes through them (as in healing a sick person); for in this latter case it is He Himself who has ordained the limiting condition: of His own will He has ordered it, that certain effects shall be produced, not by a direct exercise

of His power, but instrumentally through other agents. But He could, at the first, have arranged it otherwise; and He can (as in miracles) exchange His ordinary mode of operation for another, if reasons exist for the change. His power can only become active through His will; and therefore if it is His will to act conditionally, His power can only act thus (Litton 1960, 68).

So God can act in a sovereign manner—and yet, because he has chosen to use secondary causes, our freedom still stands. This is why we can trust God completely and know his promises to be true, yet remain responsible for our own actions. This is the answer to the question, "Why pray if God has it all figured out?" We pray because God has determined that, through our prayers, things will happen. We can act of our free will, and yet God's will shall be done. This can happen because God is infinite. Because God has infinite choices and options, he can use the actions of our free will and still direct all things as his will determines.

Maybe my favorite illustration of this will help. When my children were younger, if I said to them that I wanted their rooms to be cleaned by tomorrow—but also that I trusted them, and I was not going to check to see if they had done the work—they would be free to act or not act. If later I find unclean rooms, we can say that—even though it was my will that the rooms be clean—it was also my will that they be allowed to choose not to clean them, since my will was not to check on them. The children were secondary causes. The difference is that my options are limited at this point—but God's options are infinite. Whatever the consequences of the rooms not being cleaned, God can still bring about his desire.

God's direction of the creation in the manner we have discussed is called *providence*. It is the care of the natural world by God and the direction of rational creatures, even as they act in their freedom, so that God's will is accomplished. Providence includes God's preservation of the entire creation. Read all of Psalm 104 and see this powerful work of God, described in verses 27-30:

> They all wait for You
> To give them their food in due season.
> You give to them, they gather it up;
> You open Your hand, they are satisfied with good.
> You hide Your face, they are dismayed;
> You take away their spirit, they expire,
> And return to their dust.
> You send forth Your Spirit, they are created;
> And You renew the face of the ground.

This providence is complete and universal, as we see in Psalm 135:6:

> Whatever the LORD pleases, He does,
> In heaven and in earth, in the seas and in all deeps.

In the book of Acts, the believers gathered, and in praise for the release of Peter and John. they said, "For truly in this city there were gathered together against Your holy servant Jesus, whom You anointed, both Herod and Pontius Pilate, along with the Gentiles and the peoples of Israel, to do whatever Your hand and Your purpose predestined to occur " (Acts 4:27-28).

Such providence and Divine care is assumed in verses like Romans 8:28: "And we know that God causes all things to work together for good to those who love God, to those who are called according to His purpose." All too often, people find comfort in this verse and do not notice that this is a promise God could not make unless God is sovereign. This providence, God's sovereignty, God's omnipotence, also cannot be true except in a monotheistic setting. If there was more than one God, then none of them could make promises. If there were many gods, then any one of them might thwart the desires of another. There could be no assurance, no hope that the plans of such gods could ever come true. Even the gods would not be sure!

How could such small gods make promises like the one in Romans 8:28 or Jeremiah 31:17, where God promises hope for the future of his people and for their children? The God of the Bible is the only notion of God that makes sense. The only God big enough to be worthy of our worship and our full trust is the God who is sovereign over every bit of creation—a God who makes promises and covenants and is big enough to back up those promises, since there is no power in creation that can hold him back.

In the midst of a discussion on Romans 8:32, John Piper shows the practical side to understanding the sovereignty of God:

> The great promise of future grace, guaranteed in the logic of Romans 8:32 is that nothing will ever enter your experience as God's child that, by God's sovereign grace, will not turn out to be a benefit to you. This is what it means for God to be God, and for God to *be for* you, and for God to freely give you all things with Christ.
>
> You must believe this or you will not thrive, or perhaps even survive as a Christian, in the pressures and temptations of modern life. There is so much pain, so many setbacks and discouragements, so many controversies and pressures. I do not know where I would turn in the ministry if I did not believe that almighty God is taking every setback and every discouragement and every controversy and every pressure and every pain, and stripping it of its destructive power and making it work for the enlargement of my joy in God (Piper 1995, 116).

If this talk of providence seems foreign to you, it is not really a surprise. The notion of providence is no longer much of a part of our culture. This change has taken place in one short generation. I was reminded of this recently when, due to our technology, I was able to watch a television show from my childhood: The Lone Ranger. In the first two episodes of that 1950s show, cultural changes were clear. In the second episode, several people came together at an opportune time to stop the bad guys. Tonto made the statement that this is what the white Parson would call *providence*.

Even in that unusual setting, the understanding of providence— now seemingly lost to our culture—was clear. All the people came together with their own ideas and in response to their own free choices, and yet it was seen as God working his will. The two go together.

Jesus Claimed Omnipotence

Jesus made the claim to be omnipotent directly and indirectly in several places and in several different ways. One of the more noticeable places this is found is Matthew 28:18. The resurrected Jesus went to Galilee to meet with the remaining eleven disciples at a designated mountain. Jesus once again accepted worship, even as some seemed to struggle with doubt. Then Jesus said to them, "All authority has been given to Me in heaven and on earth. Go therefore and make disciples of all the nations, baptizing them in the name of the Father and the Son and the Holy Spirit, teaching them to observe all that I commanded you; and lo, I am with you always, even to the end of the age" (Matthew 28:18-20).

In this promise, Jesus assumed his own omnipresence and eternality, and by saying that he had all authority on heaven and earth, he claimed omnipotence and sovereignty. Some critics would call this a derived authority, since he said it had been given to him, but he was speaking in the last moments of his incarnation, where he had taken on the nature of humanity. He spoke of the kind of interaction we would expect between the Father and the Incarnate Son as the son still deals with his humanity. We see here that the kind of authority Jesus talked about was *all authority,* inclusive of heaven and earth. This is clearly only possible for an omnipotent being, and it shows that Jesus was claiming a sovereign rule over all creation.

We see omnipresence also claimed in Matthew 18:20: "For where two or three have gathered together in My name, I am there in their midst." This verse is often used as an excuse for small attendance at church meetings, but we need to see the power in it. It is a great comfort that when we gather as believers, Jesus has promised to be in our midst. But as believers gather in all places and all times Jesus must be claiming omnipresence which is the infinity of presence, just as omnipotence is the infinity of power. Can we have one without the other?

This omnipresence is another attribute of God related to sovereignty and omnipotence. This is God's infinity related to place. There is no place where God cannot be found; no place that is not full of his presence. This may sound like we are saying that God is spread out over all places, but we are saying more than that. The historic Christian claim is that God is fully in all places. All of God is everywhere. This creates a tension for us as we try to wrap our minds around this notion of the infinity of place. On the one hand God is immanent, in that God is everywhere and relates to all creation. On the other hand God is also transcendent, in that God is in no particular place. God is above and beyond and other than the creation.

Once again we see that some religions have tried to solve this dilemma by believing in small, limited gods like Zeus or Thor, or by believing in a vast, impersonal force. Yet omniscience and omnipresence are attributes Jesus claims for himself, as we have seen in Matthew 18:20 and 28:20. These attributes display both a personal nature and omnipotence: a transcendence and an immanence.

In John 15, Jesus was in the middle of a discussion on persecution and was teaching on how the believers ought to love one another because the world was not going to love them. Jesus said that we will be persecuted, just as he was. Yet he offered hope as he began to speak of the presence of the Holy Spirit in the lives of believers. As part of what became his longest discussion of the work and indwelling of the Holy Spirt, Jesus said in John 15:26, "When the Helper comes, whom I will send to you from the Father, that is the Spirit of truth who proceeds from the Father, He will testify about Me."

Jesus claimed to have the power and authority to send the Holy Spirit. As we saw in our discussion on the Trinity, the Holy Spirit is fully God and one in essence with the Father and the Son. This means that only God the Father or the Son could send the Holy Spirit. This is an act of omnipotent, sovereign deity, which Jesus again claimed in John 16:7. Some wonder why it was a benefit that Jesus would be going away, but he explained the need in this passage: "But I tell you the truth, it is to your advantage that I go away; for if I do not go away, the Helper will not come to you; but if I go, I will send Him to you."

It will benefit the church at large if the Holy Spirit comes to live with us, but connected to that hope is the promise Jesus makes to send the Holy Spirit. Who else could have the authority to command the Holy Spirit but God himself? More than this, the Holy Spirit will share and witness concerning Jesus. What he speaks will originate with Jesus. He will not speak on his own initiative "but whatever He hears, He will speak, and He will disclose to what is to come. He shall glorify me; for He shall take of Mine, and shall disclose it to you" (John 16:13-14). Jesus holds the authority to send the Holy Spirit and the Holy Spirit of God deems it his role to witness to the glory of Jesus. Jesus claims all of this for himself. It is no less than a claim to deity.

Matthew 13 is a chapter full of parables. There is the Parable of the Sower, then the Tares, followed by the Mustard Seed and the Parable of the Leaven. Then, as happens fairly often, once they get off alone, the disciples asked Jesus to explain the parables. This time, they wanted an explanation of the Parable of the Tares. This parable was an allegory; Jesus explained that the sower in this parable is the Son of Man, a reference to himself. The field is the world, and the good seed is what he called "sons of the kingdom," which established the context here as the Kingdom of God.

The tares were the opposite of the "sons of the kingdom," as they were "sons of the evil one." In giving this explanation, Jesus used his most common title as a reference to himself. In verse 41, Jesus says, "The Son of Man will send forth His angels, and they will gather out of His kingdom all STUMBLING BLOCKS, AND THOSE WHO COMMIT LAWLESSNESS."

By referring to himself, Jesus claimed that the meaning of this parable is that he will send his angels in judgment. But wait a minute! Only God can send angels, right? Yet Jesus said here that he had that power himself. We know this because Jesus himself referred to angels as "the angels of God," under sole power of God.

In Luke 12:8-9, Jesus refers to angels as being "of God" twice. "And I say to you, everyone who confesses Me before men, the Son of Man will confess him also before the angels of God; but he who denies Me before men will be denied before the angels of God." They are the angels of God, under the authority of God, yet Jesus claimed to have that authority. This is clearly a claim to sovereignty and omnipotence.

Even more than this, it is important that the setting of this discussion in Matthew 13 is the Kingdom of God. Jesus said in verse 41 that it was his Kingdom he was talking about, and yet in verse 43, he speaks of the same Kingdom in a different way: "Then THE RIGHTEOUS WILL SHINE FORTH AS THE SUN in the kingdom of their Father. He who has ears, let him hear." Jesus claimed that the Kingdom of the Father was also the Kingdom he had been speaking of. It is his Kingdom. The Kingdom of God, the Kingdom of heaven, is—according to Jesus—the Kingdom of Jesus.

So Jesus is Lord of the angels and Lord of the Kingdom of God as it is being established on earth. He is one in essence with the Father, which means it is entirely appropriate for him to claim to send the Holy Spirit. Beyond all of this, Jesus also claims to be Lord of the Sabbath.

It is clear in the Ten Commandments and other places (Exodus 23:12) that God created the Sabbath, and yet we find an interesting event in Mark 2.

In the midst of their journeys, Jesus and the disciples were walking through some grain fields on the Sabbath. As they went along, the disciples picked some of the heads of grain. The Pharisees jumped right on this and claimed it was unlawful to do such work on the Sabbath. The disciples were not stealing, and they were not reaping in any sense of that word, but none the less the Pharisees charged them with Sabbath-breaking.

Jesus gave an amazing response and challenged the Pharisee's knowledge of the Old Testament. Jesus referred to the event in 1 Samuel 21 when David and his companions ate the consecrated bread, which was only for the priests. Jesus was connecting the two events, as they both involved hunger—but even more so that they both involved doing good, which is allowed on the Sabbath. Then, in verses 27-28, Jesus explains what the Old Testament says by pointing out that the Sabbath was made for man—that is, for his rest and for his chance to worship. The Sabbath was established as a time of worship for God—and yet Jesus said that he (the Son of Man) is the Lord of the Sabbath and has the right to say what is proper on the Sabbath. The Bible tells us that God created the Sabbath, and therefore, only God is Lord of that day. Notice that Jesus was saying these things to believing Jews who knew and believed the Old Testament.

This passage raises, once again, an idea we briefly noted in the introduction: the idea of Lordship. In Luke 2:10-11, which we hear every Christmas, the angel appears to the shepherds, who were frightened by their appearance. "But the angel said to them, "Do not be afraid; for behold, I bring you good news of great joy which will be for all the people; for today in the city of David there has been born for you a Savior, who is Christ the Lord." From the very beginning, Jesus is spoken of as *Lord*.

To get a grasp of the importance of this title, we need to understand the use of the word. I am sure you have noticed that the word *sir* in English is used at least two different ways. It is used in the context of polite respect for those we speak to, and also used as a title of authority, rank, or position, as in Sir Lancelot or Sir Paul McCartney.

As we look at the title *Lord* we see that it is part of the first Christian creed found in the New Testament which was *Jesus is Lord*. Paul used it in Romans 10:9: "That if you confess with your mouth Jesus as Lord, and believe in your heart that God raised Him from the dead, you will be saved" and again in 1 Corinthians 12:3: "Therefore I make known to you that no one speaking by the Spirit of God says, 'Jesus is accursed'; and no one can say, 'Jesus is Lord,' except by the Holy Spirit."

But what kind of weight does this title for Jesus carry? Well, it might have been used in the polite, respectful sense at times, but we do not see much of that usage. The word *Lord* might also carry a bit more authority, similar to *master,* as in Matthew 21:3: "If anyone says anything to you, you shall say, 'The Lord has need of them,' and immediately he will send them." The term may also be used—and this is central to our point—as a reference to the ultimate divine authority. This is particularly so in the context of a people steeped in the worldview of the Old Testament and Hebrew culture. Berkhof sums up the historic Christian position:

> The name "Lord" is applied to God in the Septuagint, (a) as the equivalent of Jehovah; (b) as the rendering of *Adonai*; and (c) as the translation of a human honorific title applied to God (chiefly *Adon*), Josh.3:11; Ps. 97:5. In the New Testament we

find a somewhat similar threefold application of the name to Christ, (a) as a polite and respectful form of address, Matt. 8:2; 20:33; (b) as expressive of ownership and authority, without implying anything as to Christ's divine character and authority, Matt. 21:3; 24:42; and (c) with the highest connotation of authority, expressive of an exalted character, and in fact practically equivalent to the name "God," Mark 12:36-37; Luke 2:11; 3:4; Acts 2:36; I Cor. 12:3; Phil. 2:11. In some cases it is hard to determine the exact connotation of the title. Undoubtedly, after the exaltation of Christ, the name was generally applied to Him in the most exalted sense. But there are instances of its use even before the resurrection, where the specifically divine import of the title has evidently already been reached, as in Matt. 7:22; Luke 5:8; John 20:28 (Berkhof 1986, 315).

In order to avoid breaking the commandment and taking God's name in vain, the Jews replaced the name of God, Yahweh, with the word *Adonai* when they would read the Scripture. As we have mentioned, many of our translations have followed this pattern and substitute LORD for Yahweh. LORD became synonymous with the name of God. When the Septuagint translated the Hebrew Bible into Greek, it used the word *Kurios* (Lord) as both the equivalent to Yahweh as well as the word to show respect and authority. The ultimate, divine sense of the word is used of Jesus by the angel in this passage in Luke, where it is connected to the notions of Savior and Christ (Messiah).

We also see *Lord* used to refer to Jesus throughout the New Testament. Paul writes that Jesus is "Lord both of the dead and the living" (Romans 14:9) and "the Lord of glory" (1 Corinthians 2:9). In Philippians 2:11, he claims that "every tongue should confess that Jesus Christ is Lord, to the glory of God the Father." The title Lord of Lords is said to be given to Jesus at his ascension, when he returns to the Father. The name that is above all names is surely the divine use of the title.

We need also note that Jesus did not shy away from this title himself. When Thomas refers to Jesus as "My Lord and my God" in John 20:28, Jesus affirms his statement and commends his belief. There is also the discussion in Matthew 22:41-45, when Jesus asked some Pharisees their view on the Messiah. They said the Messiah, the Christ, would be a son of David. Jesus then asked them how David, under the authority of the Spirit (which tells us something of Jesus's view of Scripture), called the one who will be Messiah *Lord* in Psalm 110.

We have seen that Jesus claimed to be the Messiah. Now we see Jesus claiming that the view of the Pharisees—a view that held that the Messiah would be a descendant of David—is true but does not go far enough. It is too limiting. He is affirming himself as David's Lord, the fulfillment of Psalm 110. This is at least partly why Psalm 110:1 is the most quoted Old Testament verse in the New Testament.

The Claims of the Apostles

As we have seen the apostles clearly affirmed the Lordship of Jesus in the ultimate, divine sense of the word, which was their most common understanding of the word from their heritage. In fact, Jesus is identified by the New Testament authors as the Lord of the Old Testament (Hebrew Bible) every time they apply to Jesus Old Testament texts that speak clearly of Yahweh/Adonai. For example, in Isaiah 40:3, Yahweh is speaking through the prophet and says:

A voice is calling,
"Clear the way for the LORD in the wilderness:

Make smooth in the desert a highway for our God."

The *LORD* here is Yahweh, a clear reference to the God of Israel. Yet in Mark 1:3, Mark applies this passage to Jesus and the work of John the Baptist in preparing a way for him. We see the same thing happening in Joel 2:32:

> And it will come about that whoever calls on the
> name of the LORD
> Will be delivered:
> For on Mount Zion and in Jerusalem
> There will be those who escape,
> As the LORD has said,
> Even among the survivors whom he LORD calls.

Yet both Acts 2:21 and Romans 10:13 use this verse in a context that speaks of salvation through Jesus. He is seen as the divine LORD of this passage. Then again, in Psalm 68:18, the psalmist says,

> You have ascended on high, You have led captive
> Your captives;
> You have received gifts among men,
> Even among the rebellious also, that the LORD
> God may dwell there.

Even among the rebellious also, that the LORD God may dwell there.

The psalmist was speaking to God and about God, and the God he was speaking to was Yahweh. Then in Ephesians 4:8, Paul uses this same verse, but tells us once again that it is about Jesus and his death and resurrection.

Jesus claimed to be the One with all authority in heaven and earth, including the authority to send the Holy Spirit and the angels. When he spoke of the Kingdom of God, he spoke of it as *his* kingdom. He spoke of the Sabbath, created by Yahweh, as being under his authority. He is the divine Lord, the presence of Yahweh himself. We see this divine authority affirmed and taught by the apostles. Charles Hodge writes of the great affirmation:

> Jesus Christ is not only thus called Lord by way of eminence, but He is declared to be the Lord of lords; to be the Lord of glory; the Lord of all; the Lord of the living and the dead; the Lord of all who are in heaven, and on earth, and under the earth. All creatures, from the highest to the lowest, must bow the knee to Him, and acknowledge his absolute dominion. He is in such a sense Lord as that no man can truly call Him Lord but by the Holy Ghost. If his Lordship were merely the supremacy which one creature can exercise over other creatures, there would be no necessity for a divine illumination to enable us to recognize his authority. But if He is Lord in the absolute sense in which God alone is Lord; if He has a right in us, and an authority over us, which belongs only to our Maker and Redeemer, then it is necessary that the Holy Spirit should so reveal to us the glory of God in the face of Jesus Christ, as to lead us to prostrate ourselves before Him as our Lord and our God (Hodge 1997, 1:496).

We can find these claims all through the New Testament. In Matthew 11:27, Jesus claims authority over all things: "All things have been handed over to Me by My Father, and no one knows the Son except the Father; nor does anyone know the Father except the Son and anyone to whom the Son wills to reveal Him," In Ephesians 1:22, Paul claims that all things are under the authority of Jesus:

"And He put all things in subjection under His feet, and gave Him as head over all things to the church." It is Jesus who sustains all of creation and is coregent with the Father over all things. "And He is the radiance of His glory and the exact representation of His nature, and upholds all things by the word of His power. When He had made purification of sins, He sat down at the right hand of the Majesty on high."

But was it the early church that created this image of Jesus? Time would not allow it.

> If Jesus' divinity is a myth invented by later generations ("the early Christian community," often a code word for "the inventors of the myth"), then there must have been at least two or three generations between the original eyewitnesses of the historical Jesus and the universal belief in the new, mythic, divinized Jesus; otherwise, the myth could never have been believed as fact because it would have been refuted by eyewitnesses of the real Jesus. Both disciples and enemies would have had reasons to oppose this new truth.
>
> However, we find no evidence at all of anyone ever opposing the so-called myth of the divine Jesus in the name of an earlier merely human Jesus. The early "demythologizers" explicitly claimed that the New Testament texts had to have been written after A.D. 150 for the myth to have taken hold. But no competent scholar today denies the first-century dating of virtually all of the New Testament—certainly Paul's letters, which clearly affirm and presuppose Jesus' divinity and the fact that the doctrine was already universal Christian orthodoxy (Kreeft and Tacelli 1994, 162-163).

CHAPTER SIX

▼

THE CLAIM TO HAVE EQUAL AUTHORITY WITH SCRIPTURE

ONE WAY IN which the infinity of God expresses itself is in God's omniscience. Psalm 33:13-15 speaks in rather anthropomorphic terms, but makes it clear that there is no limit to God's knowledge.

> The LORD looks from heaven;
> He sees all the sons of men;
> From His dwelling place He looks out
> On all the inhabitants of the earth,
> He who fashions the hearts of them all,
> He who understands all their works.

It is verses like this that our parents used when they wanted to try to get us to behave: "God sees everything" they would say. But the knowledge of God's omniscience ought to be comforting as well as awesome. Part of what is meant by omniscience is that God knows all things perfectly. God is not limited to impressions or generalities. As I have said, because God is infinite, he can know you as if no other person in the world existed. What and who God knows, which is everything and everyone, God knows perfectly. God knows your unique aspects and he knows what you have in common with others. God knows our pretend motives and our real motives. This amazing aspect of God's nature has a personal side, as we see in Ezekiel 11:5, when Yahweh tells Israel that he knows their thoughts.

Omniscience allows God to be close and personal and know us in the fullest sense. When we struggle with emotional issues, or with guilt, God knows our struggle and is with us in it. "We will know by this that we are of the truth, and will assure our heart before Him in whatever our heart condemns us; for God is greater than our heart and knows all things" (1 John 3:20). God's knowledge humbles us and makes us realize our sin, but it also makes known to us God's love and compassion. As we used to sing at summer camp, the one who knows us best loves us the most.

God knows all things. He made them and he plans their course, past, present, and future. Because God is infinite, his knowledge is unbounded. In contrast to this, the idea has been proposed in recent years that God learns. This is an unnecessary idea meant to protect human freedom by involving God in the creation. Such an idea would diminish our understanding of the nature of God. For God the past, present, and future are experienced at once as present. God understands time, God created time, but God does not come to know time in the way that we, as finite creatures, know time.

We know things as we learn, building one thing upon another, moving from premise to conclusion, or just experiencing something new. But none of that happens for God. God just knows. He knows that things change but, being outside of time, he does not experience it as we do. But what about our free will? If God knows all things, including all things that will happen, then how are we finite humans free?

This brings us back to the discussion in the last chapter about our freedom and its relationship to God knowing all the possible outcomes of all things. Once again, it is important to remember that God uses secondary causes. Christianity does not teach the determinism of Islam, where God directly commands all things as they happen. God has chosen that there will be consequences to our actions, and they will make a real difference. God knows all things in advance and works out his will, given the knowledge of all possible events. So our free choices are part of what God knows and sees. These choices are free in our experience and yet are known to God and, as the sovereign One, God has planned so that our choices, in complete freedom, will bring about his will.

I have often used an illustration, which I think is a bit weak, but it seems to have helped some people understand this concept. I had a friend in college who, for the three years that our time there overlapped, never went past a water fountain without taking a drink—maybe not a big drink, but he always took a drink. After about a year of this behavior, whenever we approached a water fountain, I knew he was going to stop. I planned for it and accommodated for it. It became sort of natural.

I did not make him do it; he did it of his own free will, yet I knew in advance it was going to happen. Now I say this is weak because I am not omniscient, and I learned his actions from experience. In both ways, I am not like God. But all of this reveals, in some sense, the way a mind might know the future, even while the person acting in that future is still free to act on their will.

There is another awesome side to the omniscience of God. Because God knows all, he can judge evil with pure justice, for no circumstance is outside of his view. "And there is no creature hidden from His sight, but all things are open and laid bare to the eyes of Him with whom we have to do" (Hebrews 4:13). This is the kind of justice the prophet Amos talked about, and it can be more than frightening, but it is also good and just. As Amos says in chapter 7, there is nowhere to go to flee from God's justice: not the grave, not heaven, not the highest mountain, not the bottom of the sea. Hiding is not an option. Full knowledge means complete justice, even as he offers grace. We are not fooling God with our sin, and we are not outside of his care. Amos reminds us of the more famous passage in Psalm 139:1-12. After talking in verses one to six about how well God knows him and guides him, the psalmist continues in verse 7.

> Where can I go from Your Spirit?
> Or where can I flee from Your presence?
> If I ascend to heaven, You are there;
> If I make my bed in Sheol, behold, You are there.
> If I take the wings of the dawn,
> If I dwell in the remotest part of the sea,
> Even there Your hand will lead me,
> And Your right hand will lay hold of me.
> If I say, "Surely the darkness will overwhelm me,
> And the light around me will be night,"
> Even the darkness is not dark to You,
> And the night is as bright as the day.
> Darkness and light are alike to You.

Proverbs 15:3 again describes the presence of God and the reach of God's knowledge:

> The eyes of the LORD are in every place,
> Watching the evil and the good.

So God knows evil? Yes, God knows evil, God sees evil, God understands evil—but God does not participate in evil and God did not create evil. This may sound strange to some. If God created everything, then how can we say he did not create evil?

One of things that always needs to be pointed out when talking about the problem of evil goes back to Augustine. Augustine spoke of evil as the *lack of the good*. Evil is the absence of the good. It is a negative, a parasite. Evil depends on the good for its existence, and not the other way around. We most often even define evil things by their comparison to the good. Our language shows this: words like *disease, disagreement,* and *discomfort.* Evil is the removal of the good or the opposition to the good.

I have heard people say, "In order to show you heaven, I have to show you hell." I do not think so; it is the other way around. Evil is the privation, and so God can know evil, but not participate in it. He can understand evil and the suffering it brings, but it never taints him, because it is a negative. Evil does not have being; it is the absence of the good.

God knows all things and all possibilities, but consider this: the more one takes into account in a decision, the more wisdom is expressed. As finite beings, we cannot take all things into account when we need to decide. But if one could take all possible things into account, the result would be perfect wisdom. God, therefore, has boundless wisdom. All of God's actions will be just, and all of God's decisions will be the best possible. Such omniscience is an attribute of God alone.

Jesus spoke of such knowledge being a part of the very nature of the Father. "Are not two sparrows sold for a cent? And yet not one of them will fall to the ground apart from your Father. But the very hairs of your head are all numbered. So do not fear; you are more valuable than many sparrows" (Matthew 10:29-31). Once again, this is a point where we must challenge polytheists. The Gods of the polytheist are not omniscient. If there were even two omniscient beings, then both would know everything the other knows, and from the same perspective. They would know each other's thoughts and experience all things the same. They would, in fact, be the same mind and thus one. The idea is self-defeating. Polytheism does not really use the word *God* the same as a theist. They do not actually have any God at all—only oversized, and usually equally flawed, humans.

In all of this, we see the amazing infinity of God as it works itself out in the area of knowledge. Omniscience is hard to even grasp for a finite mind. Yet we can see that Jesus claimed this attribute for himself, even as he considered the context of his human limitations while incarnate.

The Claims of Jesus

In the first chapter of John, Jesus called his disciples: Andrew, and then Peter, and then Philip. Philip went and found Nathanael and told him about Jesus. Nathanael then made the famous statement in verse 48, "Can any good thing come out of Nazareth?" Philip challenged him to come and see.

As they approached Jesus from some distance, we see first hint of a claim of omniscience in Jesus's response to Nathanael in John 1:48: "Nathanael said to Him, 'How do You know me?' Jesus answered and said to him, 'Before Philip called you, when you were under the fig tree, I saw you.'" Here Jesus claims to know the past and to have knowledge at a distance. We might not know how far or how long Jesus was from the meeting of Philip and Nathanael, but it was far enough to deeply impress Nathanael, who responded, "Rabbi, You are the Son of God; You are the King of Israel" (John 1:49).

Jesus also claimed to know the future. Not long after the Transfiguration, Jesus was with the disciples in Galilee and he gave them a warning of some shocking events that were in his future. "And while they were gathering together in Galilee, Jesus said to them, 'The Son of Man is going to be delivered into the hands of men; and they will kill Him, and He will be raised on the third day.' And they were deeply grieved" (Matthew 17:22-23). What Jesus predicted certainly came true and displayed his knowledge of the future.

On several occasions, Jesus knew what people were thinking. In Mark 6 Jesus was in a synagogue and the scribes and Pharisees were keeping an eye on him to see if he might heal someone on the Sabbath, so they could catch him in the act. Mark tells us in verse 8, "But He knew what they were thinking." Some might say Jesus was able to tell by their presence what they were up to, but he follows up by sharing what he knew to be their very thoughts, and then he performed a supernatural healing, which irritated the Pharisees to no end.

This same supernatural knowledge was demonstrated repeatedly in the life of Jesus. In Luke 5, when an ailing man was lowered down through roof by his friends, we are told that Jesus again was aware of the thoughts of the Pharisees (Luke 5:22). In John 11, Jesus had been told that Lazarus was sick, but after the messengers had left, he told the disciples that Lazarus had died. Once again, Jesus knew what had happened at a distance. In Matthew 9:3-4, in what might be another telling of the event in Luke 5, we are told that Jesus knew the thoughts of the Pharisees. In Luke 9, the disciples were arguing among themselves as to who was the greatest among them. Jesus, "knowing what they were thinking in their heart," turned their focus toward a child standing nearby and gave them an object lesson (Luke 9:46-48).

Matthew 11:27 gives us a direct claim by Jesus to divine knowledge. "All things have been handed over to Me by My Father; and no one knows the Son except the Father; nor does anyone know the Father except the Son, and anyone to whom the Son wills to reveal Him." The first part of this claim is not unusual: No one knows the Son except the Father. That sounds like it might be said of anyone. But in the next line, Jesus attributed to himself the same kind of knowledge that he had just attributed to God. He claimed that he knew God, just as God knew him. He put himself on the same level, and in a common relationship with, the Father. By using the word *except*, he claimed a completely unique position of knowledge and relationship.

Boettner says this verse is "a declaration in which Jesus Himself implies that the personality or being of the Son is so great that only

God can fully comprehend it, and that the knowledge of the son is so unlimited that He can know God to perfection; in other words, a declaration that His knowledge is infinite" (Boettner 1960, 162).

Jesus also described his divine relationship in Luke 22:29, where he spoke of God the Father granting him a kingdom. He goes on to talk of Satan's demand for permission to sift Peter like wheat. Jesus said that he had prayed for Peter, and then goes on to predict Peter's betrayal, right down to the crowing of the cock. In this same chapter, Jesus had called Peter and John to prepare the Passover. They wanted to know where to go, and Jesus told them that when they entered into the city, they would meet a man carrying a pitcher of water and he would lead them to the right house. It all happened just as Jesus said. Then in verse 21, Jesus made a bold prediction: "But behold, the hand of the one betraying Me is with Me on the table." All of this should not have surprised them, because on the previous Sunday, Jesus had sent two disciples into town, telling them just where and how they would find a donkey. He even told them what to say if someone were to ask about them taking it. "And those who were sent went away and found it just as He had told them" (Luke 19:32).

Even more so in Luke 7:37-59, we see two things that reveal the divine nature of Jesus's knowledge. Jesus was at the home of a Pharisee. A woman enters the house and begins to anoint Jesus's feet with perfume and wet his feet with her tears, then wiping them with her hair. The woman apparently had a reputation, and the Pharisee knew of her. The Pharisee said to himself that if Jesus were a prophet, he would have known what kind of woman this was. The man said this to himself—yet Jesus answered him as if he knew the man's very thoughts. Then, as Jesus forgave the woman's sins—which he seemed to know all about, even though he did not know the woman—he forgave on the basis of her faith, displaying that he knew what was in her heart.

All of this is similar to Jesus meeting the Samaritan woman at the well in John 4. Jesus told her things about her marriage that revealed knowledge beyond what any human could have known, and then went on to predict the future of worship, which would move beyond both Jerusalem and Mt. Gerizim. The woman was amazed and called others to see this man who "told me all of the things I have ever done" (John 4:29).

Now there are a couple of verses which raise questions about the omniscience of Jesus. Matthew 24:36 is the one most often brought up by critics. Speaking of the time when heaven and earth would pass away, Jesus said, "But of that day and hour no one knows, not even the angels of heaven, nor the Son, but the Father alone." It certainly seems to say that there is something Jesus does not know.

In Luke 8:45, when a woman reached out and touched Jesus's cloak, he turned and asked: "Who is the one who touched me?" Now we can see that it is quite possible, and it fits the context, that Jesus was just asking so the woman would identify herself. It was for the benefit of her faith and not for his knowledge that he asked the question. But the passage in Matthew 24 takes us a bit deeper.

The theme of Matthew is that Jesus is fully God, but we must not forget that he was also fully human. When we consider the combination of the two, it can help us understand this difficult concept. A strong parallel is the relationship in each of us between the body and the soul. We might say Bob is tall, and we might say Bob is kind. His height has to do with Bob's body, and his kindness has nothing to do with Bob's body—yet both can be true of Bob. That which is fully God in Jesus might be omniscient, and that which is fully human in Jesus might not be; but both are true of Jesus. There might be times when Jesus was speaking of his divine nature and other times when he spoke of his human nature. One does not cancel out the other.

Charles Hodge explained all of this very clearly:

> We may predicate of the man whatever may be predicated of his body; and we may predicate of him

whatever may be predicated of his soul. We may say of the man that he is tall or short; that he is sick or well; that he is handsome or deformed. In like manner, we may say that he is judicious, wise, good, benevolent, or learned. Whatever is true of either element of his constitution is true of the man. What is true of the one, however, is not true of the other. When the body is wounded or burnt it is not the soul that is the subject of these accidents; and when the soul is penitent or believing, or enlightened and informed, the body is not the subject spoken of. Each has its properties and changes, but the person or man is the subject of them all ... The union of soul and body in the constitution of man is the analogue of the union of the divine and human nature in the person of Christ. No analogy is expected to answer in all points. There is in this case enough of resemblance to sustain faith and rebuke unbelief (Hodge 1997, 2:379-380).

We have already seen that Jesus claimed and used the attribute of omniscience on a number of occasions. How could he seem to lack information at other times? Could it be that Jesus, by an act of his will, could choose to respond from his divine nature or his human nature? Could it be that the knowledge of when his return would be was not for humans to know—and so, in his divine wisdom, he chose not to reveal this information to us by accessing his divine knowledge? Perhaps it was knowledge meant to stay between him and the Father in their eternal relationship.

As the second person of the Trinity, Jesus would never be ignorant of anything, as he is one in essence with the omniscient nature of the Father. But Jesus, in the incarnation, has taken on a fully human nature, which is capable of change. His human body and nature grew and matured. He felt human needs. In John 4:6, we are told he was tired. In Matthew 4:2, Jesus was hungry. Most famously, in Luke 2:52, we are told, "And Jesus kept increasing in wisdom and stature, and in favor with God and men." All of these changes could only be true of Jesus's human side.

That Jesus is fully human and fully divine is central to the Christian faith. We see it working itself out here as Jesus spoke from his human side, revealing that some things are not open to the knowledge of humans: one of these is the day of his return for judgment. The point of Jesus's words in the context of Matthew 24 is that we need to be ready: "Therefore be on the alert, for you do not know which day your Lord is coming." Not knowing the day is important for both us and for Jesus. Jesus chooses, then, not to make that information available. As the incarnate one, he may access the divine nature or not. By an act of his will and obedience, he chose to follow the will of the Father and not receive or communicate this knowledge, primarily for our sake.

The Apostolic Testimony

The apostles saw the omniscience of Jesus and confessed it. In John 16:30, Jesus was preparing the Apostles for his death and eventual return to the Father. It was with this information in mind that they made a confession "Now we know that You know all things, and have no need for anyone to question You; by this we believe that You came from God." They had become aware of, and confident of, Jesus's omniscience. It had been at least part of what brought them to faith.

The Apostles reaffirm here what John had shared earlier in his Gospel. Even as Judas betrayed him, Jesus had known from the beginning who would not believe in him. "'But there are some of you who do not believe.' For Jesus knew from the beginning who they were who did not believe, and who it was that would betray Him." (John 6:64). The betrayal of Judas brought about another statement concerning Jesus's knowledge and especially his knowledge of the future. Judas had begun his betrayal and the soldiers were on their way to arrest Jesus. "So Jesus, knowing all the things that were coming upon Him, went forth and said to them, 'Whom do you seek?'" (John 18:4).

In John 2:24-25, we see Jesus early in his ministry. He had performed his first miracle at the wedding in Cana and had moved on to Jerusalem for the Passover. At Jerusalem, Jesus cleansed the temple for the first time and gave a prophecy of his own death and resurrection. John commented that many were believing in Jesus because of the signs he was doing. But John went on to mention that Jesus, "on His part, was not entrusting Himself to them, for He knew all men, and because He did not need anyone to testify concerning man, for He Himself knew what was in man." So we see that, even though Jesus did not always express his divine omniscience while incarnate, he did act in a way that the apostles saw him as having supernatural knowledge.

At the end of the first chapter of his letter to the Colossians, Paul had begun to share what he had been going through in his attempts to proclaim the gospel to the Gentiles. Then, in the first three verses of chapter 2, he told the readers his motivation:

> For I want you to know how great a struggle I have on your behalf and for those who are at Laodicea, and for all those who have not personally seen my face, that their hearts may be encouraged, having been knit together in love, and attaining to all the wealth that comes from the full assurance of understanding, resulting in a true knowledge of God's mystery, that is, Christ Himself, in whom are hidden all the treasures of wisdom and knowledge.

Paul had already affirmed the deity of Jesus in the first chapter by affirming that all the fullness of God dwells in Jesus. In this passage he then affirmed that all wisdom and knowledge dwelt in Jesus, as he affirmed Jesus's omniscience before once again proclaiming his deity in verse 9.

In Hebrews 1:6-8, we see the author of Hebrews beginning the argument for the greatness of Jesus by saying that Jesus is greater than the angels. In speaking of the Son, the author looked back to the Old Testament.

> And when He again brings the firstborn into the world, He says "AND LET ALL THE ANGELS OF GOD WORSHIP HIM." And of the angels He says, "WHO MAKES HIS ANGELS WINDS, AND HIS MINISTERS A FLAME OF FIRE." But of the Son He says, "YOR THRONE, O GOD, IS FOREVER AND EVER, AND THE RIGHTEOUS SCEPTER IS THE SCEPTER OF HIS KINGDOM."

Jesus claimed the authority equal to the Scripture as the revelation of God. Those who knew him saw the same authority as part of his very being: an eternal authority above the angels—the very Word of God in their presence.

Jesus's View of Scripture

It is our claim that Jesus recognized his divine omniscience, and that one way he displayed this omniscience and affirmed his deity was to make his words equal with Scripture. It will help if we take a moment to see that Jesus believed the Hebrew Scriptures were the divine words of God. Therefore, if he made his words equal to the Hebrew Scriptures, then he was claiming equality with, and the omniscience of, Yahweh.

Jesus made many references to Old Testament events while always assuming them to be factually true. I have combined some of the available lists of these references over the years, and I will add the Scripture references for further study. Jesus mentions, always with the presumption of their reality, all of the following:

Abraham (Matthew 3:9; 8:11), Noah (Matthew 24:32-39; Luke 17:26-27), Sodom and Gomorrah (Matthew 10:15), Sodom alone (Matthew 11:23; Luke 10:12; 17:29), the Prophets and their suffering eleven times (e.g. Matthew 23:37; Luke 6:23; 13:34), David eating the showbread (Matthew 12:38), Solomon (Matthew 6:29), Elijah (Matthew 17:11), Jonah (Matthew 12:41), David as the author of Psalms (Mark 12:36), Abel (Luke 11:51), Lot (Luke 17:28), Isaac and Jacob (Luke 13:28), Elisha (Luke 4:27), Zechariah (Luke 11:51), Moses as lawgiver eight times (e.g. John 1:17), manna (John 6:31), Moses raising the serpent (John 3:14), circumcision seven times (e.g. John 7:22).

The references to Abel and Zechariah are particularly interesting because he refers to them in the same verse and would appear to imply the covering of the whole Hebrew Bible, since Abel appears in the first book and Zechariah appears in the last book.

We can also see Jesus using the Hebrew Bible and trusting its doctrine and teachings. At his temptation in Matthew 4, Jesus responded to the temptations of Satan by quoting the Old Testament. He seemed to think it was enough, and it worked. When Jesus was asked about the greatest commandment, he did not make up a new one, but rather quoted again from the Old Testament (Matthew 23:37-40). When a young man asked Jesus about how to obtain eternal life, Jesus used the words of the Old Testament to answer him and challenged him to become a follower (Matthew 19:18-19).

Jesus criticized the Pharisees for letting tradition stand in the way of Scripture. After quoting from Isaiah, he said, "Neglecting the commandment of God, you hold to the tradition of men" (Mark 7:8). It would seem that for Jesus, the Old Testament was the authority in matters of salvation, and this was, at least in part, because the Old Testament pointed to him. He made this clear in John 5:39-40: "You search the Scriptures because you think that in them you have eternal life; it is these that testify about Me; and you are unwilling to come to Me so that you may have life."

We find that Jesus never rebuked anyone, not even the Pharisees, for studying or believing the Old Testament. He did, however, criticize them for not obeying Scripture (Matthew 22:29; 23:23; Mark 12:24). The Scripture was so important to Jesus, and he held it in such high regard that, on the very day of his resurrection, he spent time expounding the Scripture and explaining it to two of his followers on the road to Emmaus. "Then beginning with Moses and with all the prophets, He explained to them the things concerning Himself in all the Scriptures" (Luke 24:27).

There is one other way Jesus affirmed that the Scriptures are the very word of God. It might be called the *dual authorship* idea. This is the Bible's view of itself. There are places where the Bible says something like "the Scripture says," but when you look up the passage, it is God speaking. Galatians 3:8 says that Scripture spoke to Abraham, but the passage quoted from Genesis 12:3 is in fact God speaking. Romans 9:17 says Scripture speaks, but it quotes Exodus 9:16 in which is God speaking to Pharaoh.

We see this same idea in the Old Testament. For instance, in Jeremiah 25 it was the Word that came to Jeremiah. Jeremiah did the speaking on behalf of the other prophets, but he speaks directly as from God: "'Yet you have not listened to Me,' declares the LORD [Yaheweh]." In these passages and others, what the Scripture says God says, and what God says the Scripture says. The origin of Scripture is from God, through humans. In Hebrew it is called the *dabar Yahweh*, the word of God.

Jesus made these same kinds of statements connecting Scripture to the very word of God. In Matthew 19:4-5, Jesus said, "He who created said" and then quoted from Genesis. Quoting God and Genesis is the same thing. In Mark 7:8-13, Jesus spoke of what the Commandments said—what Moses said—and then refers to both as the word of God. In Mark 12:36, Jesus said that David spoke by the Holy Spirit, which shows the two sides of this dual authorship. In John 10:34, Jesus quotes from the Psalms, but refers to it as the Law. All Scripture is binding in Jesus's view: it all comes from God. This is why, as we look at Jesus's claims about his word being equal with Scripture, we see that this is a claim to deity: his word is God's word.

But how does the New Testament fit into all of this? Obviously, Jesus did not have the New Testament—but did this view of authority carry over to the writing of the New Testament? Historic Christianity has claimed that both the authority and the inspiration carried over. First, we can see a promise made to the apostles by Jesus in John 14:26: "But the Helper, the Holy Spirit, whom the Father will send in My name, He will teach you all things, and bring to your remembrance all that I said to you." Then Jesus added to this promise in John 16:13: "But when He, the Spirit of truth, comes, He will guide you into all the truth; for He will not speak on His own initiative, but whatever He hears, He will speak; and He will disclose to you what is to come." This promise is what the apostles claimed had happened in the prophets and was now going to happen through them:

> As to this salvation, the prophets who prophesied of the grace that would come to you made careful searched and inquiries, seeking to know what person or time the Spirit of Christ within them was indicating as He predicted the sufferings of Christ and the glories to follow. It was revealed to them that they were not serving themselves, but you, in these things which now have been announced to you through those who preached the gospel to you by the Holy Spirit sent from heaven—things into which angels long to look (I Peter 1:10-12).

Peter makes the connection with the prophets and Paul claims the same direct work of the Spirit for his words and thoughts. "Now we have received, not the spirit of the world, but the Spirit who is from God, so that we may know the things freely given to us by God, which things we also speak, not in words taught by human wisdom, but in those taught by the Spirit, combining spiritual thoughts with spiritual words" (2 Corinthians 2:12-13).

This was clear enough to the apostles that, even before the New Testament was completed, they were referring to each other's writing as Scripture. In 2 Timothy 5:18, Paul quotes two passages he calls Scripture. One is from Deuteronomy but the second—"The laborer is worthy of his wages"—is from Matthew 10:10 and Luke 10:7. There is also the well-known passage in 2 Peter 3:14-16, where Peter refers to the writings of Paul as Scripture. He also admits that some are hard to understand:

> Therefore, beloved, since you look for these things, be diligent to be found by Him in peace, spotless and blameless, and regard the patience of our Lord as salvation; just as also our beloved brother Paul, according to the wisdom given him, wrote to you, as also in all his letters, speaking in them of these things, in which are some things hard to understand, which the untaught and unstable distort, as they do also the rest of the Scriptures, to their own destruction..

Jesus's view of Scripture carried over to the New Testament, but what is important for our discussion is that he saw the Scripture he had—the Law, the Prophets, and the Writings (the *Tanakh*, or Hebrew Bible)—as having been spoken by God. So when he makes his words equal with Scripture, he is claiming to be the God who inspires Scripture.

Jesus's Divine Knowledge Equal with God's Word

Judaism looks back to Moses as a great leader, as do Christians. But the book of Hebrews tells us of Jesus's superiority over Moses, saying things like, "Now Moses was faithful in all His house as a servant, for a testimony of those things which were to be spoken later; but Christ was faithful as a Son over His house whose house we are, if we hold fast our confidence until the end" (Hebrews 4:5-6). Also in 2 Corinthians 3, we see a reminder of Exodus 34, where Moses put a veil over his face to tone down the reflected glory of God. Jesus claimed to actually *be* that glory. In all of the claims we have spoken of, in all of the ways that Jesus displayed himself as God with us, there is the inherent claim that he bears the authority of God.

We all remember that Jesus had a low opinion of hypocrisy, and so it has become a favorite way for unbelievers to mock Christians. Remembering what hypocrisy is helps us, at this point. Hypocrisy is pretending to be something you are not. Hypocrisy is not failing at what you are trying to be. Many critics fail to see that not reaching the standard God has set for us is sin, but it is not hypocrisy. Claiming that we have reached some level of holiness, when we have not, is hypocrisy (and a sin). If someone claims to be perfect and they are not, which we can count on, then they are a hypocrite. But admitting that one is not perfect, and therefore in need of a savior, is the way one becomes a Christian. Christians claim that there is a standard that needs to be met. as we serve a holy God. To set that standard high before us and then not to reach it is sin, but it is not hypocrisy. We are not perfect; we are, as eighteenth-century Methodist Church founder John Wesley said, going on to perfection.

Given all of this, to say that Jesus was impersonating God, or pretending to be God, to accommodate his culture would be a gross misunderstanding of his own claims and values. Seriously, if impersonating a law enforcement officer is a crime, how serious would it be to impersonate God? Jesus would be both a liar and a hypocrite—and yet these are the very things his teaching and his life tell us are *not* part of his being. How could we respect such a person? We make fun of people acting like more than they are. We see Barney Fife waving his gun when we know the bullet is in his pocket, and we laugh. Stories like the one about the golfer who complained to his caddy to stop looking at his watch because it was distracting, and the caddy responding with "This isn't a watch, it's a compass" are funny because they bring down to size someone who thinks they are more than they are. How could we take Jesus seriously if he claimed to be God, and carry with him therefore the authority of God, if in fact he was not God? It is exactly this authority that Jesus claims for himself. It is something Moses would never have claimed.

In Matthew 24:35, Jesus made his words equal with the words of God when he said, "Heaven and earth will pass away, by My words shall not pass away." Now we might not think that this statement by itself is a claim to equal authority with God's word. However, we need to put this statement in the context of what Jesus had already said in Matthew 5:18: "For truly I say to you, until heaven and earth pass away, not the smallest letter or stroke shall pass away from the Law until all is accomplished." Jesus used the exact same language to describe the authority of his words and the authority of God's words.

These lines from the Sermon on the Mount are not the only place in that passage where Jesus revealed this connection. In several places in Matthew 5, Jesus referred to the teaching of the Old Testament. He began by saying, "You have heard ..." and then continued, "But I say to you..." Jesus then moved on to build upon the original teaching. Notice that Jesus did not change or challenge the original teaching when it was from Scripture. He did challenge a couple of sayings that were tradition, or the teaching of the Pharisees, but he did not challenge the Scripture text itself— and in fact, he made it even more authoritative, as he taught how it covers motive and not just action. So he placed his authority above the Pharisees and the traditions. He put his authority on the level of the Scripture, the word of God.

We see this same authority being expressed in Matthew 28:18. This was at the end of Jesus's earthly ministry. He had risen from the dead and spent forty days with his followers. Now, just before he was to leave them to return to the Father, Jesus gave them some final words, starting with: "All authority has been given to Me in heaven and on earth." As we saw earlier, some try to make the point that the claim of Jesus in this passage was that he had been given authority when, if he were God, he would always have had authority. But Jesus may have been claiming the fulfillment of Daniel 7:13-14 at this point.

Daniel 7:13-14 refers to one like the "Son of Man," which is a phrase used in the gospels eighty-one times for Jesus. As we saw in chapter 2, it was Jesus's most common title for himself. But this "Son of Man" comes on the clouds—something we see only God do in the Old Testament (Psalm 18:9-10; 104:3 and Isaiah 19:1). The "Son of Man" is God exercising his authority on earth, and Jesus claimed that authority.

Jesus had already used this language in Matthew 24:30 when he spoke of the end of time when the Son of Man would come in the clouds with power and glory and the authority to dispatch the angels. This is consistent with the stance Jesus took earlier in Matthew, where we see that Satan challenged the authority of Jesus. Yet when Jesus answered, he said we shall not tempt the Lord our God. If Jesus was the one being challenged and tempted, and yet he makes the point that we are not to tempt God, then he was making his divine nature clear in the very face of Satan.

In another claim to authority, Jesus did something that we hardly notice. Early in Jesus's ministry, he was calling the twelve to be his disciples. Andrew, who had heard John the Baptist speak and who had spent the day with Jesus, brought his brother Simon to Jesus. In John 1:42, Jesus changed the name of Simon to Peter. We might not notice anything overwhelming here, but because God changed Abram's name to Abraham and Jacob's name to Israel, it was understood that only God had the authority to change someone's name. Jesus assumes this primary authority without a second thought. Remember, the prophets always held a secondary authority and said many times, "Thus saith the LORD." Jesus acted and spoke differently. He often said "Truly, truly I say unto you." That is why in John 7:46, they say, "Never did a man speak the way this man speaks."

Then, in John 13:34, we see that it was the night of the Passover and Jesus was sitting at table with the apostles at what we refer to as the Last Supper. Judas had just left to betray Jesus. Then Jesus began to teach the other apostles. Here were a group of men who knew that Moses had given the commandments and that the Old Testament Law had come from God through Moses. Jesus spoke with the authority to give a new commandment: "A new commandment I give to you, that you love one another, even as I have loved you, that you also love one another." Jesus spoke as one who had the authority to add to the commandments, to add to Scripture. As Hodge said, the authority and the truth found in Jesus are bound together. As the omniscient one, Jesus is the final authority.

> Everything which He declared to be true, all Christians have ever felt bound to believe, without examination; and all that He commanded to do or to avoid, they have ever regarded as binding the conscience. His authority is the ultimate and highest ground of faith and moral obligation. As the infinite and absolute reason dwelt in Him bodily, His words were the words of God. He declared himself to be the Truth, and therefore to question what He said was to reject the truth. He was announced as the [Logos], the personal and manifested Reason, which was and is the light of the world—the source of all reason and of all knowledge to rational creatures. Hence He spake as never man spake (Hodge 1997, 1:499-500).

▼

CHAPTER SEVEN

THE CLAIM TO HAVE THE POWER OF LIFE AND DEATH

CREATIVITY IS A part of our life. I am often amazed at the creativity of people, for good, for beauty, and for evil. It seems we are naturally creative, and historic Christianity gives a reason for our creativity. It tells us that we are created in the image of a creative God. We are then meant to be, as Tolkien taught, sub-creators as we live in the image of the creator (Tolkien 1966, 3). We can get creative without even thinking about it. It seems to come naturally, even in our speaking. I heard once of a Quaker man here in Pennsylvania who, some time ago, found a man trying to break into his safe. The Quaker grabbed his gun, and while aiming at the man said, "I would not hurt you, but you are standing where I am about to shoot." Even threats can be creative.

Often when we think of creation we think of the creation/evolution debate but that is not what we want to discuss in this chapter. In connection with some of the ideas we discussed in chapters 2 and 3, we'll focus on some concepts that are important if we are to understand the Christian idea of God as Creator, and how the claims of Jesus connect to that idea. First, we want to notice that the creation was an act of the Trinity. In 2 Corinthians 8:6, Paul says, "Yet for us there is but one God, the Father, from whom are all things and we exist for Him; and one Lord, Jesus Christ, by whom are all things, and we exist through Him." Here we see that all things exist because of an act of the Father and the Son. Jesus is said to be active in creation. Do not miss the obvious parallel that Paul is making here between the Father and the Son. Jesus and the Father are described with the same words and seen as taking the same actions. Part of what John wants us to understand is that Jesus, as the Word, is active in the creation.

In the prologue to his gospel, John tells us, "All things came into being through Him, and apart from Him nothing came into being that has come into being" (John 1:3). In this passage, John is telling us that Jesus is the Word and, as the Word, all things came into being through him. It has always been amazing to Christians that this follows closely with the understanding of Genesis that God *spoke* the creation into being. Looking back on Genesis 1:1-2, Christians can see the vastness of creation as the act of God the Father. This creative act was done through speaking (the Word) even as the Spirit of God moved over the creation. If God the Father is the actor in creation, then this would make any claims or hints Jesus gave about being part of the act of creating, or of having authority over the creation, a claim to deity.

Second, we notice that God created as an act of his free will. It seems obvious in the Genesis account that God was acting on his own free will, since there was no one and nothing there to influence him until he started creating. Revelation 4:11 openly states that God was acting on his own behalf. "Worthy art Thou, our LORD and our God, to receive glory and honor and power; for Thou didst create all things, and because of Thy will they existed, and were created." So there was nothing outside of God the Father,

Son, and Holy Spirit that took part in the creation. Therefore, to claim to be part of the act of creation, or to claim authority over the creation, is to claim to be God.

Just to be clear, when we talk of this creative act we are talking comprehensively. That is, God created *all things* that exist outside of himself. It is here that we see potential confusion over the language, "firstborn of all creation." "And He is the image of the invisible God, the firstborn of all creation. For in Him all things were created, both in the heavens and on earth, visible and invisible, whether thrones or dominions or rulers or authorities—all things have been created through Him and for Him. And He is before all things, and in Him all things hold together" (Colossians 1:15-17).

It might sound like Jesus is less than God in the first part of this passage. Is he just an image of God? Maybe he is only the first created being, as the Jehovah's Witnesses teach. But the word *image* here, given the context of what Paul has just said about Jesus forgiving sins and being the beloved Son, is reminding us of the fullness of the incarnation. And, as Jesus said, if we see the Son, we see the Father. Jesus made the invisible God visible to us and is, in that sense, the image of God.

Being the firstborn of creation is a bit more serious. But, to review from chapter 3, the words *first born* and in other places *only begotten* (*prototokos* and *monogenes*) convey an imagery from the Old Testament that includes the idea of a first son, but it also conveys, and is often used to describe, a child who holds a special place: a unique child. It is a term of honor, not a term of birth order or of being created. As we have seen, in Hebrews 11:17, we are told that Abraham was asked to offer up his only begotten son, Isaac. But Isaac was not the first born of Abraham—Ishmael was. *First born* was a title of honor and relationship, and an expression of love. This is the connection being expressed here between the Father and the Son. The Son is not created, he is unique and is ultimately the Creator. The heart of what we want to see in the above passage in Colossians is that God has created all things and that Paul here tells us that this comprehensive work was done by Jesus.

Before we look at more ways Jesus is connected to the creation, it is important for us to see why the idea of God creating makes such a big difference. This doctrine gives value and importance to the creation for several reasons. First, nothing in the creation is an illusion or an accident, which means that everything that exists has value—including you as an individual. The material world was made because God desired it, and it was pronounced good. God loves all he created, and so should we. Sin has corrupted the creation, but the creation has not lost its value.

Second, as we noted above, God made us in his image, which includes creativity. There is value to human achievement, work, thought, art, and music, all because we are displaying the nature God has given us. Third, we see again that God works through secondary causes. He allows the creation to function as he created it to. It's not that he is unable to break into the creation, but that he allows his orderly universe to function and he makes use of secondary causes. His will shall always be done, but he is able to achieve that will using human freedom and creativity. This is the foundation that gives our work, and all of our living as his creatures, value.

Fourth, the creation of God gives a reason for science and knowledge in general. We live in an orderly universe, not a random one—so science can exist. Scientists can experiment and trust its results. Science emerged in a Biblical worldview, and Christians should be the best scientists. Fifth, the doctrine of creation is a strong reminder that all things derive from God and therefore, only God is worthy of worship. False gods are no gods at all, and worshiping any part of the creation makes no sense when we can worship the Creator. Paul explains this in 1 Corinthians 8:4-6 as he sets the stage for the verse we looked at above:

> Therefore concerning the eating of things sacrificed
> to idols, we know that there is no such thing as an
> idol in the world, and that there is no God but
> one. For even if there are so-called gods whether in

heaven or on earth, as indeed there are many gods
and many lords, yet for us there is but one God, the
Father, from whom are all things and we exist for
Him; and one Lord, Jesus Christ, by whom are all
things, and we exist through Him.

Unlike the other attributes we have looked at, Jesus does not
make a direct claim to be the Creator. Yet who he was, what he
did, and what he said made the Apostles quite certain he was, in
fact, the Creator.

In Colossians 3, Paul talks about our new life in Christ. He
speaks of the Christ who now sits at the right hand of God; the one
in whom our life is hidden. We are to put on Christ and bear the
image of the one who created us. "Do not lie to one another, since
you laid aside the old self with its evil practices, and have put on
the new self who is being renewed to a true knowledge according
to the image of the One who created him" (Col. 3: 9-10).

Now it could be said here that this act of creation is only about
the spiritual "new self," but it would seem that the next verse—
which mentions various races, nationalities, and social positions—
is including the whole person. The author of Hebrews is even more
open about the Son's role in creation. While the focus in the opening
verses of Hebrews is about God speaking to us, and how that has
happened in many ways throughout history, the notion that the
final word is now in Jesus becomes central. It is Jesus, the Son, who
is lifted up. He has the final word because he is the one through
whom God made all things. "God, after He spoke long ago to the
fathers in the prophets in many portions and in many ways, in these
last days has spoken to us in His Son, whom He appointed heir of
all things, through whom also He made the world" (Hebrews 1:1-2).

The Apostle John was convinced of Jesus's role as Creator. In
verse 1 of John 1, the Apostle affirms the deity of Jesus and his
presence from eternity: "In the beginning was the Word, and the
Word was with God, and the Word was God." Some, particularly

the Jehovah's Witnesses, would deny this verse teaches that Jesus is God. They claim that, since the Greek language does not use the article before the word for God, it must mean a lesser god. They claim that if there is no article, it must always mean someone other than Jehovah (Yahweh) God.

Without going into a lot of Greek grammar, a couple of illustrations will help. In Luke 1:35, Mary was being told by the angel that she was about to have a son who would be called the Son of God. There is no article here before the word *God* and so that would make the phrase mean the Son of a lesser God. But Jesus is that lesser God, according to the Jehovah's Witnesses, and that would make this verse mean Jesus was his own son. Philippians 2:11 refers to "God the Father," but uses no article. If no article means it is not Jehovah (Yahweh), then in this verse, Jehovah is not the Father, and we are left without anyone being God the Father.

A number of other examples can be found, but John 20:28-29 gives a reverse clue. In these verses, Thomas referred to Jesus and called him God. In this case, the article is used—and so, by the logic of the Jehovah's Witnesses, Jesus is called God (Jehovah) in this passage. All of this shows that Jesus truly is spoken of as God in John 1:1, and the grammar is clear. With that understanding, the stage is set for John 1:10: " He was in the world, and the world was made through Him, and the world did not know Him." Jesus—who John saw as equal with, and coexistent with, the Father—is said here to have made all things. So God is the Creator, yet Jesus is the One through whom all things came into being. Jesus is that God, and as God, Jesus has the power over life and death: a power he claims for himself.

Jesus Claims the Power of Life and Death

Because God is the Creator, God has the power over life and death. There was no hiding this in the Old Testament. In Deuteronomy 32:39, Yahweh says:

> See now that I, I am He
> And there is no god besides Me;
> It is I who put to death and give life.
> I have wounded, and it is I who heal;
> And there is no one who can deliver from My hand.

Then, in the famous Prayer of Hannah in 1 Samuel 2:6, we read, "The LORD [Yahweh] kills and makes alive; He brings down to Sheol and raises up." Even Job, in the middle of his struggles, acknowledges that his life comes from God:

> Thou hast granted me life and lovingkindness;
> And Thy care has preserved my spirit (Job 10:12).

The psalmist cannot help but see all life as coming from God. In Psalm 127, children are praised as a gift from Yahweh, "like arrows in the hand of a warrior" (verse 4). The man is blessed, it says, who has a quiver full of them. I remember being struck by these verses many years ago when I worked at a summer camp. Part of my job was to teach archery, and as I read these verses, I went straight to the shed and filled my quiver, which held thirty two arrows. I thought, "A quiver full of children? I don't think so."

Psalm 139 is often cited because of its reverence for life given by God. We must note that it also speaks of our days being ordained and limited by God:

> For Thou didst form my inward parts;
> Thou didst weave me in my mother's womb,
> I will give thanks to Thee, for I am fearfully and
> wonderfully made;
> Wonderful are Thy works,
> And my soul knows it very well.
> My frame was not hidden from Thee,
> When I was made in secret,

And skillfully wrought in the depths of the earth,
Thine eyes have seen my unformed substance;
And in Thy book they were all written,
The days that were ordained for me,
When as yet there was not one of them.

Then, looking back on the sacrificial system of the Old Covenant, the author of Hebrews points out that death is appointed to us, that it only happens once, and then comes judgment. God is in control of the whole system that brought us to the time of Christ, and God will use his death and ours to show the power of resurrection. "And inasmuch as it is appointed for men to die once, and after this comes judgment" (Hebrews 9:27). It is God who determines life and death. It is exactly this power that Jesus claims for himself.

In John 5:21-29, Jesus affirmed in several places his power over life and death—the same power possessed by God the Father. In verse 21, "For just as the Father raises the dead and gives them life, even so the Son also gives life to whom He wishes." Jesus then claimed to be the One who will render final judgment, but added that hearing and believing his words will bring eternal life and an avoidance of judgment. "Truly, truly, I say to you, he who hears My word, and believes Him who sent Me, has eternal life, and does not come into judgment, but has passed out of death into life." Jesus claimed his very words were life-giving. Then Jesus became even more specific, claiming to bring life, to raise the dead, and even to grant eternal life. When he claims to be the one who brings life and death, he is claiming to be God.

Jesus said in John 5:25-29:

Truly, truly, I say to you, an hour is coming and now is, when the dead will hear the voice of the Son of God, and those who hear will live. For just as the Father has life in Himself, even so He gave to the Son also to have life in Himself; and He gave Him authority to execute judgment, because He is the Son of Man. Do not marvel at this; for an hour is coming, in which all who are in the tombs will hear His voice, and will come forth; those who did the good deeds to a resurrection of life, those who committed the evil deeds to a resurrection of judgment.

Later, in John 10, Jesus again connected hearing his voice with his giving of life and life eternal. In Jerusalem, at the time of the Feast of Dedication, Jesus was once again debating with those around him. They asked how long it would be until he made clear who he was. The crowd wanted him to tell them plainly whether he was the Messiah. Jesus responded, "My sheep hear my voice, and I know them, and they follow me: and I give eternal life to them, and they shall never perish; and no one shall snatch them out of My hand" (John 10:27-28). All the power lies with the Shepherd who will give eternal life, and who has the power to protect that life from all opposition.

In the very next chapter of John, Jesus demonstrated his authority over death with the raising of Lazarus. But before that happened, Jesus made one of his most famous claims as he attempted to console Lazarus's sister, Martha. She affirmed that Jesus could have kept Lazarus from death. Jesus claimed that her brother would rise again, and she assumed he meant on the last day, at the great resurrection. Jesus both corrected her and assured her in 11:25-26: "I am the resurrection and the life; he who believes in Me shall live even if he dies, and everyone who lives and believes in Me shall never die. Do you believe this?"

Some might question if Jesus really claimed to have power over life and death, since the verses we have looked at speak mostly of eternal life. Could this have been just a spiritual message, and not really a claim of authority over physical life and death? But this passage is just one that reveals the claim clearly has to do with physical life and death. Not only did the words of Jesus speak of physical life and death, the context of the raising of Lazarus made the point with clarity.

There are other places where Jesus displayed this power over life and death. In Luke 7, Jesus came to the city of Capernaum and was asked by a Centurion to save the life of a slave who was near death. Jesus responded to the Centurion's faith and healed the slave. Soon after this, Jesus was approaching the gate to a city called Nain and he took things a step further. He saw a procession coming out carrying a dead man who was the only son of a woman walking with the crowd. Jesus comforted the woman and then touched the coffin as the bearers stopped. Jesus spoke, and the man was raised and began to speak. Then Jesus presented him back to his mother.

The witnesses were overwhelmed at this display of power over death. Did Jesus mean for these acts to display who he was as God with us? It seems that he did, for the very next thing in Luke 7 is a discussion with the followers of John the Baptist. John's followers asked, on behalf of John, if Jesus was the One they were looking for. Jesus told them to go tell John what they had seen: the healings and the raising from the dead. Here was the evidence Jesus offered in order to show that he was God in their presence.

Jesus continued to demonstrate this power in front of his apostles. In the next chapter, Luke 8, we see Jesus raising the daughter of Jairus. Jairus had come to Jesus asking for his daughter to be healed, but then learned that she had died. Jesus once again offered comfort and took with him Jairus, along with Peter, James, and John. Now the people who were tending to the girl were not ignorant or superstitious. When Jesus made the claim that the girl was not dead, they laughed at him—but then they were stunned when he spoke and the girl's spirit returned and she came back to life. Mark tells us the girl was twelve years old and immediately got up and walked (Mark 5:22-43).

The Apostolic Claims

The followers of Jesus understood the power of Jesus over death, especially after his resurrection. They bound our life, and life eternal, to his life and resurrection. By faith, we unite with him and share in the consequences of his work. Paul tells us, "For if we have become united with Him in the likeness of His death, certainly we shall also be in the likeness of His resurrection, knowing this, that our old self was crucified with Him, in order that our body of sin might be done away with, so that we would no longer be slaves to sin" (Romans 6:5-6).

Both death and life are found in our connection to Jesus. Paul also sees this as a connection of the Son to the other two persons of the Trinity. "But if the Spirit of Him who raised Jesus from the dead dwells in you, He who raised Christ Jesus from the dead will also give life to your mortal bodies through His Spirit who dwells in you" (Romans 8:11). Paul continues to connect the life and death of the believer to Jesus when he looks ahead to Jesus's future return. He ties together the life and death of believers with the resurrection and the rapture, and it is all based on our being united to Christ.

In 2 Timothy 1, Paul told Timothy of God's plan through history and his gift of faith to everyone who becomes part of the church, and reminded him of how all of this had happened through Jesus and the grace he brought. God's plans have been from eternity, "but now has been revealed by the appearing of our Savior Christ Jesus, who abolished death and brought life and immortality to light through the gospel" (2 Timothy 1:10). It seems the authority of Jesus over life and death is closely related to his bringing of salvation by his conquering death and establishing eternal life for all who believe.

In Revelation chapter 1, we see a claim by Jesus as seen in the vision of John—so, in a sense, it is both the claim of Jesus and the claim of the Apostle. John's vision had begun. He said he "was in the Spirit on the Lord's day" (Revelation 1:10). He heard a loud sound like a trumpet, but it was a voice. Then he saw a vision of Jesus, in which he described, in magnificent terms, Jesus as the Son of Man. John portrayed him just as the Ancient of Days is portrayed in Daniel 7:13 and the divine glory is revealed in Ezekiel 1:26.

In the presence of this glory, John fell to the ground. "When I saw Him, I fell at His feet like a dead man. And He placed His right hand on me, saying, 'Do not be afraid; I am the first and the last, and the living One; and I was dead, and behold, I am alive forevermore, and I have the keys of death and of Hades'" (Revelation 1:17-18). Jesus here claimed the title of Yahweh that was used earlier in the same chapter in verse 8: "first and last" compared to "Alpha and Omega." He also claimed here to possess the power of death and its results, even as he claimed to have defeated death, which showed he had the power of life.

The Gospel of John gives us even more evidence. In looking at the High Priestly Prayer in John 17, Charles Hodge reminds us of Jesus's teaching in John 14-16, in which he promises to send the Holy Spirit to be with believers after he leaves. Of the prayer of John 17, Hodge says, "His intercessory prayer could proceed from the lips of none but a divine person. He speaks as one who had power over all flesh, and who could give eternal life to all who God the Father had given Him. Eternal life consists in the knowledge of God, and of Him who God had sent" (Hodge 1997, 1:508).

The Issue of Justice

The claim to have the power over life and death once again raises the issue of justice. We could point out that, if Jesus claimed to be God, and justice is an attribute of God, then all of Jesus's decisions concerning life and death would be just. When people question the justice of God, we could say that all creation is God's and God can do whatever he pleases with that creation—but that explanation does not quite ease people's minds. It is true that God is ruler over all creation, and he has created a just, moral standard as he governs the creation. There is a standard because there is a God.

When we talk about the justice of God, and the just way Jesus would hold dominion over life and death, we are talking about the way the holiness of God is expressed in relation to moral, personal beings. Theologians call this a *distributive justice* because it describes the way God hands out rewards and punishments. If there were no evil, there would be no punishment. So justice is the working out of God's holiness and righteousness and a clear demonstration of his opposition to evil.

As moral beings, we are held to the standard of the moral perfection of God. God's justice is how God deals with our failure to live up to that standard, and he does so either through judgment or grace. We break that standard by the acts of our own will. Our inclination is to be our own God, and we bow to that inclination—yet God is always just and even more than that, merciful, but never unjust. We also see in Scripture that this justice is applicable to both individuals and nations. Jesus spoke of the individual response in Matthew 22:12-14, in the conclusion of the parable of the wedding feast, and in Matthew 25, in the parable of the ten virgins and the parable of the talents. Yet in Matthew 11, starting in verse 20, Jesus spoke of judgment on the cities of Chorazin, Bethsaida, and Capernaum.

What we have seen here is several aspects of the justice of God. Theologians like to name everything— names and definitions do make communication easier—and so we see each of these aspects summed up by Calvinist theologian Anthony Hoekema:

> By God's rectoral justice, we mean God's rectitude as the Ruler of the Universe, particularly of His moral creatures. By His distributive justice, we mean His rectitude in the execution of His law. In this connection, we think first of God's remunerative justice, which distributes rewards

not on the basis of merit but solely by grace. Paul speaks of this in Romans 2:6 and 7: "Who will render to every man according to his work: to them that by patience in well-doing seek for glory and honor and incorruption, eternal life." By retributive justice, we mean God's infliction of penalties upon those who disobey Him; this justice is an expression of His wrath (Hoekema 1974, 32).

Jesus has authority over life and death because he is God. This is a comfort, not a fearful thing, because this authority incorporates the justice of God. It does not always seem that God's justice is being worked out in the world. Things do not always seem fair or just in this life, which, oddly enough, is an idea some have used as an argument for an afterlife. From Thomas Aquinas to C. S. Lewis and Peter Kreeft, philosophers have argued that all of our natural desires can be fulfilled in this life, even if some are not. Therefore desires such as justice—which are not fulfilled in this life—point to a fulfillment in another life. However this argument works out we can at least say that it is not a good idea to evaluate the eternal justice of God based on the experience of one limited lifetime.

All of this talk about life and death, judgment, and justice does raise again the struggle of understanding the connection between love and justice. Many people today want to talk only of the love of God. They claim to have an example in Jesus of that pure love—love with no judgment. But, as we saw in the introduction, the attributes of God, Father, Son, and Holy Spirit are not in conflict with each other. These attributes actually exist together in perfect union with each other. Love includes justice. How could one be loving and unjust at the same time? And so love is not merely granting wishes and creating warm feelings; love is doing what is right for someone, even if what we do doesn't make them feel better about the situation. There is no conflict here, and Jesus is the perfect representation of this. The justice of God requires that there be a penalty for sin, but the love of God is shown by Jesus paying that penalty, so we may live.

Jesus's claim to have power over life and death is an assertion that he is the Creator. This is not all there is to the claim, however. Jesus displayed his power over the creation by performing miracles. Miracles backed up his claim to be Creator. To substantiate this claim, we would need to defend his miracles and, even more basically, defend miracles in general. This we will do in the next chapter.

▼

CHAPTER EIGHT

THE CLAIM OF MIRACLES AS EVIDENCE

AS WE MENTIONED earlier, John the Baptist sent disciples to ask Jesus if he was the coming messiah, or should they look for someone else. Jesus answered them with a claim that his miracles were evidence of who he was. "And He answered and said to them, 'Go and report to John what you have seen and heard: the BLIND RECEIVE SIGHT, the lame walk, the lepers are cleansed, and the deaf hear, the dead are raised up, the POOR HAVE THE GOSPEL PREACHED TO THEM'" (Luke 7:22).

The gospels tell us that Jesus performed a number of miracles, from healing and raising the dead to feeding 5,000 people, walking on the water, and calming a storm. The life of Jesus was bracketed by miracles at the beginning and end: virgin birth, resurrection, and ascension. Jesus claimed that his miracles gave evidence of his divinity, of his presence as Messiah. Miracles do not always prove divinity. God did miracles through others in the Bible:

Moses, Joshua, Elijah, Elisha, Samson, Jonah, Peter, and Stephen, for example. But, as we will see, miracles confirm a messenger of God, and Jesus's message was that he *is* God. Therefore the role of miracles is important as part of Jesus's self-claims to deity. Notice also that there is a dramatic difference between Jesus and others who did miracles in the Bible. Moses and the prophets and the apostles performed miracles—or more correctly, God did miracles through them—and such was exactly their claim: that it was God working through them.

When Moses, the prophets, or the Apostles wrought miracles, they expressly disclaimed the idea that it was by their own efficiency. "Why look ye on us, says the Apostle Peter, as though by our own power we made this man whole?" (Hodge 1997, 1:503). But Jesus claimed that his miracles were done through his own power. Only God could have the power to enter into and effect the creation in the ways Jesus did.

Jesus performing miracles and the coming of the Kingdom of God seem to be closely tied together in Jesus's teaching. In Luke 1:20, Jesus said, "But if I cast out demons by the finger of God, then the Kingdom of God has come upon you." Healing was also connected to Jesus bringing in the Kingdom. Matthew 3:23 tells us, "Jesus was going throughout all Galilee, teaching in their synagogues and proclaiming the gospel of the kingdom, and healing every kind of disease and every kind of sickness among the people." Jesus brought the Kingdom of God with him. He told the apostles to go out to heal and serve because the kingdom of God was near them. And so, because Jesus is himself the presence of the Kingdom of God, he can perform miracles as the One who has authority in that Kingdom.

> And whatever city you enter and they receive you,
> eat what is set before you; and heal those in it who
> are sick, and say to them, 'The kingdom of God
> has come near to you." But whatever city you enter

and they do not receive you, go out into its streets
and say, "Even the dust of your city which clings
to our feet we wipe off in protest against you; yet
be sure of this, that the kingdom of God has come
near" (Luke 10:8-11).

Jesus was amazed that people could witness these miracles, and
even admit that they had seen them, and still not believe. Mark 6:1-6
tells us Jesus was teaching in his home town of Nazareth. In verse
two, the people admitted that he had done miracles—and yet they
still doubted. This caused Jesus to wonder at their unbelief. And yet
the signs and wonders Jesus performed did have an effect on many
of the people who witnessed them, and they did reveal his Deity, as
many observers responded in awe. But we must admit that the very
existence of miracles demands some defense in our day.

First of all, it is a bit difficult to define a miracle. Some,
like British philosopher Anthony Flew, might say, "A miracle is
something which would never have happened had nature, as it
were, been left to its own devices" (Flew 1967, 346). Peter Kreeft
and Ronald Tacelli define a miracle as "a striking and religiously
significant intervention of God in the system of natural causes
(Kreeft and Tacelli 1994, 109). They also go on to point out two
important ideas about miracles. One is that miracles do not deny,
but actually assume, that nature is basically an orderly and self-
contained system of cause and effect. If nature did not act in a
regular fashion, then there would not be the possibility of notable
exceptions. They also point out that a miracle is not a contradiction.
Jesus's walking on the water was not a contradiction. Jesus walking
on the water and *not* walking on the water at the same time would
be a contradiction.

Another example of a definition for a miracle is stated by
American theologian Norman Geisler: "A miracle is an act of God
to confirm the word of God through a messenger of God" (Geisler
1999, 450). This definition helps with our current discussion on the

divinity of Jesus and also explains the inspiration of Scripture. It also helps us deal with issues like the questions of false miracles and whether or not Satan can perform miracles.

Biblically, miracles must possess three traits, as described in Acts 2:22: "Men of Israel, listen to these words: Jesus the Nazarene, a man attested to you by God with miracles and wonders and signs which God performed through Him in your midst, just as you yourselves know." The first trait, translated here as *miracles,* is the Greek word for *power.* The power for a miracle comes from God, who is transcendent over the creation. The power is not merely magical or mystical. Second we see *wonder.* A miracle inspires awe and astonishment in those who observe it, not just curiosity. Third is the word *sign.* A miracle is a sign, a testimony to authenticate God's messenger and message.

This knowledge helps us respond to a question asked even by believers. When a miracle occurs, how can we know it is from God? Could it be from some evil spirt or demon, or even Satan? Well, first of all, does it confirm a messenger of God? Satan can only mislead and pretend. Look at the context of the event. Does the miracle do good? Does it draw people closer to God? Does it glorify God? Does it contradict the revelation of God in Scripture? Since God is good, no true miracle can be evil.

When holding that miracles are possible there are a number of issues that require further affirmations. One such affirmation is that the people in Biblical times knew what they were talking about. This is in response to the sometimes mocking claim that the people back in Bible times just didn't know any better. This claim points out what C. S. Lewis called "chronological snobbery." People today think the people in those days just were not as educated as us and not as aware as we are. Maybe they just didn't know that things like miracles were not normal. This idea is often couched in academic language. Some have claimed that all the healings in the Bible were psychosomatic and not miraculous, but the people just did not know any better.

Yet we must ask, if people in Biblical times did not know that water does not usually part, that people cannot walk on water, that babies are not born to virgins, that dead people do not rise, that water does not turn into wine, and that storms do not obey human commands—then why would they have had any reason to call these events miracles in the first place? They would have no framework in which to recognize these events as miracles. If they did not know the natural way in which these things usually happen, they would not have assumed a miracle when they happened differently, and they would not have assumed divine help. You have to know the natural laws to believe and recognize a miracle.

Another affirmation that seems to surprise people is that a belief in miracles does not require going against the scientific method. We do not have to give up science. It is certainly true that science depends on the regularity of the universe. Science studies an orderly universe where we can expect the laws of nature to hold up in all situations—a foundation of order that originally came from a Biblical worldview, we might add. The cause of that order, the reason for existence, why there is something rather than nothing, the existence of God and miracles, and many other questions might all be valid—but because they are not testable, they might be beyond science. This does not mean, however, that they are contrary to science.

Science, by its own methodology, can study what *is* and cannot study what is *not*. It can study what has happened, but not what has not happened. Certainly science can extrapolate from what we know to what we do not know. Science can create theories. But if we are talking about a specific event or action, then trying to prove it *could not happen* would involve proving a negative, and the skeptic is on difficult ground at that point. The skeptic might then fall back on a philosophical argument called *naturalism*, which simply denies the possibility of miracles.

More to the point, when we are talking about a miracle, we are not trying to find out if the same thing would happen again if the conditions were right: that would be science. We are trying to find out if it happened on this one occasion: that is history. When looking at the resurrection, we are not asking if men usually rise from the dead, or could ever again rise from the dead; we are asking if Jesus did rise, on this one occasion. That's history, not science.

One cannot prove or disprove the supernatural by using natural tests. So we are not denying the scientific method; we are saying it is not the method to use in this area of study. It is not equipped to tell us if there are miracles. Philosophy can show that miracles are possible. Theology and the nature of God can show that miracles are probable. History would show that miracles are actual. All of this would start with the understanding that creation, itself, is a miracle.

We need to be careful here when someone philosophically presupposes that miracles cannot happen and then implies that science agrees. But if someone assumes miracles cannot happen, before they study the evidence for the event they are denying, then they are not being scientific. It is not very good science to reach a conclusion before looking at the evidence.

It is true that the primary evidence for miracles has been eye witnesses. Some, like Scottish philosopher David Hume (Geisler 1984, 279), have suggested that there is not enough evidence to substantiate miracles because not enough people saw them (and because those who did see them lacked integrity). The question then is, how many would it take? The New Testament tells us that a room full of religious leaders, including opponents of Christ, saw a paralytic healed. Is that enough? The resurrected Christ was seen by more than 500 people. Is that enough? Between 5,000 and 15,000 people, including women and children, were fed at once with just a small basket full of supplies. Is that enough? Along with this the evidence that the Biblical manuscripts are trustworthy would work against the argument that the witnesses lacked integrity.

Other critics might claim that miracles are just random events in a random universe. This kind of response to the idea of miracles arises often in dialogue and debate. But this response actually denies science more than the idea of miracles. It takes away the orderly structure of the universe and says that anything could happen at any moment, by chance. Science would not be possible under such a system of thought. Coming out of the post-modern view that there is no truth—along with chaos theory and New Age irrationalism—the notion emerges that, given an infinite amount of time and an infinite universe, anything could happen. You can see more about the infinite time idea in the Appendix.

So, why can't miracles be just another unusual occurrence in a random universe? In a world where there is no truth, anything might happen, especially given enough time. There are those who hold that what we call miracles are just a result of things we do not yet understand. They don't deny that these things happen, but they see no reason to assume that miracles are from God. They are supernormal, not supernatural. Maybe miracles are just things we could do, and probably will do in the future, once we learn our full human potential.

This view does away with miracles by redefining them and bringing them into the realm of the natural. It says that nothing that happens can be a miracle, because if it actually happens, it isn't a miracle. This defining away of miracles by definition is also done in a more philosophical way. Geisler gives us one example from a critic of miracles, philosopher Alistair McKinnon:

> McKinnon's argument can be summarized as follows: 1. Natural laws describe the actual course of events. 2. A miracle is a violation of natural law. 3. But it is impossible to violate the actual course of events (what is, is; what happens, happens). 4. Therefore miracles are impossible (Geisler 1999, 452).

McKinnon and other naturalists attempt to define away miracle by simply saying anything that happens is not a miracle. This is not an answer to the possibility of miracles. It in fact begs the question. Geisler goes on to show the problems with this argument. The definition of *natural law* is too strong. It would be better defined as what regularly happens. Since natural law deals with regular events, and a miracle is an irregular event, they are two different classes and cannot be compared. Author Dinesh D'Souza describes this well:

> When we have subjected a theory to expansive testing, and it has not been falsified, we can provisionally believe it to be true. This is not, however, because the theory has been proven, or even because it is likely to be true. Rather, we proceed in this way because, practically speaking, we don't have a better way to proceed. We give a theory the benefit of the doubt until we find out otherwise. There is nothing wrong in all of this as long as we realize that scientific laws are not "laws of nature." They are human laws, and they represent a form of best-guessing about the world. What we call laws are nothing more than observed patterns and sequences. We think the world works in this way until future experience proves contrary (D'Souza 2007, 187).

Christians would also affirm that miracles do not say anything negative about God. One of the arguments made against the idea of miracle is that God's intervention implies that God created the universe and did not quite get it right, and so has to tweak it a little here and there. This might be a valid criticism if we were defending a Deistic view of the universe, where God just created everything and then let it go on its own. It would be a true statement if God had created the universe in such a way that he never planned to intercede.

This is theoretically possible. God could have created a universe where he did not need to answer prayer, reveal himself, or intervene in any way. If God had done this, and then had to step in on occasion, that would mean God had not done a perfect job. But if God's intention and plan was to act in the history of the creation from time to time, then God has done exactly what he intended. Then looking at this from the perspective that God actually exists, we must say that there would then be nothing in the nature of God to suggest that he would not, or could not, perform miracles. If God exists, and is omnipotent, then God is able. Whether God would, or has, performed miracles is a different question—but there is no reason to presuppose that God could not or would not perform them.

Some might be surprised to learn that Christians also affirm that miracles do not violate the laws of nature or the uniformity of nature. Now, if by the uniformity of nature one means the uniformity of natural causes in a closed system, then we must respond that such an idea assumes the question at hand. The question we are dealing with is whether the natural world is a closed system, or can God intervene in that system. If we define the system as closed, it is like saying that miracles violate the idea that miracles can never happen.

Our claim is that miracles do not *violate* anything. God would only be violating the laws of nature if they were above God and he was obligated to obey them—but it is the other way around. God has the authority and the right to modify God's creation, and there is no guilt or impropriety in this. Nothing is violated.

As I write this, the Corona virus has caused the school where I teach to change to online classes. This was not a violation of any laws or rules, and especially not of the rights of the professors or students, because the administration had the authority to make that change. It is true that the laws of nature are true if there is no interference. This is good and Biblical and something we count on each day. For example, using the laws of nature, physics etc., we can predict the course of a ball if, and only if, no unknown interference comes into play. But even if you jump out from a hiding place and hit the ball off into some new direction, the original laws are still valid and accurate. There was just another factor those laws could not take into account. This is what we claim for miracles: they are the ultimate outside force.

> If I put six pennies into a drawer on Monday and six more on Tuesday, the laws decree that – *other things being equal*—I shall find twelve pennies there on Wednesday. But if the drawer has been robbed, I may in fact find only two. Something will have been broken (the lock on the drawer or the laws of England) but the laws of arithmetic will not have been broken. The new situation created by the thief will illustrate the laws of arithmetic just as well as the original situation (Lewis 1947, 58).

We have noted that, if God exists, there is nothing in the nature of God that would suggest that he would not or could not perform miracles. In the same way, when we look at nature, we see nothing that precludes the possibility of God's intervening in that nature. This is so especially if God created that nature in the first place. If God can do the miracle of creating the whole thing, then God can do the smaller miracle of intervening as he sees fit. If God is the author of the universe, can he not write into it any plot twist he chooses?

It might help us to remember that the laws of nature do not cause anything—they are descriptions of how things usually happen, and therefore laws are not broken when a miracle occurs. In fact, the Christian worldview would claim that we need to be careful not to make a false division between the natural and the supernatural. We need to avoid falling into the trap of thinking that the universe runs itself on natural laws most of the time, and that God jumps in only on occasion. Read Psalm 104 and you will see that God is in control of both the ordinary and extraordinary. We have seen Psalm 135:6 earlier, but notice what it says around this verse:

> For I know that the LORD is great,
> And that our Lord is above all gods.
> Whatever the LORD pleases, He does,
> In heaven and in earth, in the seas and in all deeps.
> He causes the vapors to ascend from the ends of
> the earth;
> Who makes lightnings for the rain,
> Who brings forth the wind from His treasuries
> (Psalm 135:5-7).

Remember this claim from Colossians 1:16-17? "For by Him all things were created, both in the heavens and on earth, visible and invisible, whether thrones or dominions or rulers or authorities—all things have been created through Him and for Him. He is before all things, and in Him all things hold together." Notice God creates, through the Son, and holds all things together. God is constantly active in the creation. God works through all of creation to bring about his will for his people, including the fallen, evil, and broken parts. "And we know that God causes all things to work together for good to those who love God, to those who are called according to His purpose" (Romans 8:28). If God was not omnipotent, he could not make this promise. If God was not active in the creation, he could not make this promise. This means miracles are not a violation of any laws; they simply refer to God's *unusual* actions as compared to God's *usual* actions in the real world.

The Issue of Truth

Jesus said that miracles were part of the evidence that he was telling the truth when he claimed to be God. In fact, Jesus claimed to be The Truth. We are claiming that miracles are real, that Jesus claimed to have performed them, and that Jesus taught us the truth in all of his teaching.

Truth has become an important issue in our world. In our day, people will mock you if you even hint that you know what God has said, even if it is clearly in Scripture. The charge often comes with anger: "Who are *you* to tell us what God says?" Somehow, people get the idea that we are claiming authority, when all we are doing is passing on the message. "Do you have a secret connection to God?" people mock. No, it is not a secret. You can have it, too. Nobody has a corner on the truth, but everyone has access to it. That is our claim.

All discussions about religion change, the stakes become higher, and the consequences are more dramatic when we grasp the claim that Jesus is the very presence of God made real and visible to this world. On the authority of Jesus, we proclaim his name above every name. So, when Moses wrote that God spoke the creation into existence, Jesus was that Word. Moses knew and loved the *dabar Yahweh*, the word of God, and Jesus is the word.

We are claiming that Jesus is "the way, and the truth, and the life" (John 14:6) in a world where truth is said to no longer exist: a world where any claim to truth in any absolute sense is seen as an attempt to oppress others. It is said that everyone may have their own truth and all ideas are equally valid (except the politically incorrect ones). But is this true? "Any society, however sincere, that believes in the equality of all ideas will pave the way for the loss of good ones ... One of the symptoms of a society that has lost its ability to think critically is that intricate issues are dealt with in a simplistic manner" (Zacharias 1996, 85).

Feelings are often seen as more important than ideas, and more valid. The result is that, when one defends a position by way of ideas, the response is often made on the basis of emotion. You might even be accused of being a bigot for not feeling the way they do. Ravi Zacharias shows us the current situation: "Truth is possibly the most violated concept in our world ... this is probably the first time, certainly in Western civilization, that a society at large does not believe in the existence of absolute truth" (Zacharias 1996, 212).

Into this culture, we proclaim that Jesus is the truth, and that he possesses the authority of God and of God's word. We proclaim this because that is what he claimed to be.

I have often said that when I began defending the Christian faith, back in the 1970s, one could look first at the evidence for God and the truthfulness of Christianity. Today, one often has to begin by defending the idea of whether truth is even knowable. Even back in 1987, American philosopher Allan Bloom made the famous statement that, "There is one thing a professor can be absolutely certain of: almost every student entering the university believes, or says he believes, that truth is relative" (Bloom 1987, 25).

The Christian worldview stands against the notion of relativism and the absence of truth. Philippians 4:8 tells us to think on whatever is true. The psalmist said to God, "The sum of Thy word is truth" (Psalm 119:160). However, the ideas of Jacques Lacan, Jacques Derrida, Michel Foucault, and others have filtered down into popular culture, so that we now hear phrases like "What may be true for you is not necessarily true for me," "Truth is relative," "Whatever works," "There are no absolutes," "Who are you to say that one view is true and another false?" This is how British social critic Os Guiness describes our culture's way of thinking:

> There is no truth, only truths. There are no principles, only preferences. There is no grand reason, only reasons. There is no privileged civilization (or culture, beliefs, periods, and styles), only a multiplicity of cultures, beliefs, periods, and styles. There is no universal justice, only interests and the competition of interest groups. There is no grand narrative of human progress, only countless stories of where people and their cultures are now. There is no simple reality or any grand objectivity of universal, detached knowledge, only a ceaseless representation of everything in terms of everything else (Guiness 1994, 105).

Living in a time when such thinking is common creates a challenge for the Christian faith. How do we communicate that Jesus is the truth, and that God's word is true, to those who do not believe in truth? John 4:24 tells us that, "God is spirit; and those who worship Him must worship in spirit and truth."

The historic, Judeo-Christian position is that God actually exists—not that we have conceived of God or imagined God, but that God is actually there and that this is a truth that is true for all people in all places in all times, and that this statement corresponds to reality. Being true for all people, in all places, and in all times is what we mean by absolute truth. If God exists, then there is absolute truth, starting with the truth that God exists.

Rather than absolute truth, some like to speak in terms of objective truth. Using the word *objective* is valid but can lead to misunderstanding. It helps to notice three things we do not mean by objective truth (Kreeft and Tacelli 1994, 363). First, when we talk about objective truth the word *objective* does not mean unemotional or detached. Objective truth has to do with the content of what we know, not our feelings or commitment as we know it. Second, objective truth does not mean that a truth is known by everyone or that it is believed by everyone. No matter who knows it or who denies it, or how many know or do not know, truth is still truth. Third, objective truth does not necessarily mean a truth that has been demonstrated to the world. Peer review is a great check on claims to truth, but truth is not dependent on acceptance by others.

I am sitting at a wooden desk as a type this. That is an objectively true statement, and it does not need to be known or confirmed by anyone else to be true. Objective truth is simply truth that is independent of the knower. All of this is important because, as we attempt to defend the nature of Jesus or any other foundational Christian belief, the arguments and evidence we submit is often met with the response, "Well, that might be true for you, but not for me." This kind of response, based on a relativistic worldview, would make all reasoning and rational thought impossible. Yet people still use this objection to avoid the consequences of argumentation and a reasoned defense of the Christian faith. Often, I hear the old parable of the blind men and the elephant used to deny truth or at least our knowledge of the truth. Norman Geisler explained it in a powerful way:

> Many people will tell you that all truth is really true from a certain way of seeing things or perspective. The old story of six blind men and the elephant is often used to illustrate and support this position. One blind man, feeling only the trunk, thought it was a snake. Another discovered only the ears and concluded that it was a fan. The one who came across the body said that it was a wall and, after finding a leg, another said it was a tree. Another holding the tail declared it was a rope. Finally, the last blind man felt a pointed tusk and informed them that it was a spear. To some, this proves that what you think is true is only a matter of your perspective of things. It should be pointed out, though, that all of the blind men were wrong. None of their conclusions were true, so this illustration says nothing about truths. There really was an objective truth that all of them failed to discover. Also, the statement, "All truth is perspectival," is either an absolute statement or a perspectival one. If it is absolute, then not all truths are perspectival. If it is perspectival, then there is no reason to think that it is absolutely true—it is only one perspective. It does not succeed either way (Geisler 2001, 257).

Sometime ago, while on a college campus here in Pennsylvania, I unexpectedly found myself having a discussion with a member of the Hare Krishna group. I always remember this discussion because, no matter what I said—even when I directly contradicted him— he said that we were in agreement. No matter what I said I believed, he said I could still believe it and be part of the Hare Krishna movement. Even when I said I could not follow Krishna or accept anything good old A.C. Bhaktivedanta Swami Prabhupada said, he said we agreed. How do you have a conversation with someone who accepts both sides of a contradiction as true?

As this kind of thinking becomes common, we must always be looking for claims that are self-refuting. When someone says there is no such thing as truth, we must ask them if they believe *that* statement to be true. The claim that there is no truth obviously puts them on the horns of a dilemma. On the one hand (or horn), if the statement is true, they have contradicted themselves. On the other hand (or horn), if the statement is not true, then why did they say it and why should we listen? We also must ask the person making this claim if we ought not to be teaching that there is such a thing as absolute truth. If the say "yes," then the question becomes, where does the "ought" come from? If there is no truth, on what basis are they able to make the claim that we are mistaken? I submit that the idea that there is no truth is held only under certain circumstances (usually academic), and only at certain times. It can be held in a classroom, but an hour later, when the wrong change is given at McDonalds, suddenly truth matters.

Some try to avoid the question of truth by saying it is merely a western way of looking at things. We in the west, they say, want to look at things as an *either or* rather than the eastern view of *both and*. "One of the most fallacious ideas ever spawned in Western attitudes toward truth is the oft-repeated pronouncement that exclusionary claims to truth are a Western way of thinking. The East, it is implied, is all-inclusionary. This is patently false" (Zacharias 1996, 221).

If my Hare Krishna friend got the wrong change at an Indian restaurant, or if someone in India got the wrong change at an American restaurant, both would claim that there was an error.

Neither would walk away saying that both their view of what they should get back and the view of the cashier are correct. Yet this kind of subjectivism is all around us.

People from all sorts of backgrounds want to say that truth is whatever makes you feel good or is emotionally satisfying to you. But some serial killers are emotionally satisfied by what they do. How can this be a criterion for truth? We need to be careful here; we are speaking against subjectivism, not subjectivity. Certainly, some things are subjective. I do not like macaroni and cheese, and you do. (I know that virtually makes me un-American.) I like The Moody Blues, and maybe you do not. But even these truths are absolute in one sense. It is true for all people in all places and in all times that Allyn Ricketts does not like macaroni and cheese and does like The Moody Blues. Many things may be subjective, but subjectivism is a worldview that is not much more than relativism with feelings. If all things are subjective, how would we even communicate? Nothing I say might mean the same thing to you. Truth cannot be only what makes us feel good or is emotionally satisfying. Bad news can be true.

To go another direction, some have said that only what we can work out and prove by reason is true. Rationalism says that truth is deductive and based on reason alone. Again, we have a self-defeating claim. It cannot be proven by reason alone that only what can be proven by reason is true. So rationalism is self-defeating: it cannot live up to its own claim, and it cannot speak to other avenues to truth.

To be sure, logic and reason are important for finding and knowing truth. There is not enough logic and rational thought going around these days. In fact, many seem to want to deny logic or rational thought as a means to knowing truth. But one must assume the laws of logic to argue for, or against, the truthfulness of the laws of logic. You cannot defend the law of non-contradiction without using the law of non-contradiction. It is not rational thought that we would speak against, but rationalism. However, if subjectivism and rationalism do not work as worldviews, then maybe we can know truth by what we experience through our senses. But if truth is just what I experience through my senses, are we not back to some kind of subjectivism or relativism?

Again, it is true that what we can experience through our senses might be true. In fact, I would claim that a Christian epistemology is the foundation for trusting our senses. But as a worldview, this empiricism fails because some things we sense are not true. There are optical illusions, mirages, hallucinations, and more. I have visited a number of people in nursing homes and hospitals who were seeing things that were not there. There are also things that we know which do not depend on our senses for their truthfulness, such as mathematics and much of philosophy and metaphysics.

All of these attempts at a worldview that would give us a true picture of reality seem much too abstract to some. They want to be more practical, and so we also find people who say truth is "whatever works." Being practical is good. Having common sense is good; we could use more of it. But defining truth by "whatever works" does not *itself* work. This pragmatism is a uniquely American-based philosophy associated with William James. We love to be practical, but it must be said that what is true is not always practical.

St. Augustine's mother's name was Monica. That fact is true, but it's of little or no practical value. Sometimes being honest and telling the truth can get us into a lot of trouble! Try telling your boss that his suit is ugly. Then again, what is practical is not always true: a lie might accomplish your goal, and cheating on a test might actually get you a good grade.

In affirming absolute and objective truth, we are not denying that a plurality of ideas might exist, or that some things are opinion or a matter of taste. We are not denying that some things appear differently from different perspectives, or that one's experience may find various truths of relative importance. We are saying that, beyond all these things, there are truths that are true for all people in all places and all times. Truth is real. People differ, and cultures differ, and these differences are important—but, "We have reversed Jesus's order. We have made truth relative and culture supreme and have been left with a world in which wickedness reigns" (Zacharias 2000, 46).

This takes us back to the "Who are *you* to tell us?" critics. It is central at this point to understand that, in claiming that there is absolute truth, we are not yet claiming anyone is wrong about anything. We are just saying there *is* truth. Without truth, everyone is open to manipulation and, in fact, manipulation is all there is if there is no truth. It needs to be made clear that when we, as humans, make the claim that there is absolute truth, that claim includes the notion that the one making the claim is also under that truth. It is not necessarily an attempt to have power over someone. The person making the claim is also subject to that truth.

We have claimed that Jesus is God and that this idea is true. We have seen that Jesus himself claimed to be the truth, and he displayed who he was by the use of miracles. Jesus is not one among many. "I am the way, and the truth, and the life; no one comes to the Father, but through Me" (John 14:6).

CHAPTER NINE

▼

CONCLUSION

IN THESE CHAPTERS, we have looked at the nature of God and the ways in which Jesus claimed to be the God of the Hebrew Bible. We have seen Jesus claim the nature of God and accept worship while knowing that only God is worthy of that worship. We have seen Jesus claim the name Messiah and accept that title when others called him Messiah. In his life he claimed, and displayed by his actions, that his was the love of God for the creation.

Jesus claimed to be judge of the world, a right only God can assume because it is based on God's holiness. Jesus claimed the sovereign rule of God and, in a Jewish setting where everyone saw the Sabbath as holy and instituted by Yahweh, Jesus claimed to be Lord of the Sabbath. Jesus pointed to his own omniscience even in the context of his incarnation and human nature. He saw his words as equal to the Scripture and, as such, they carried the authority of God. Jesus claimed the power over life and death and established his power over the creation by raising the dead and performing miracles.

There are other ways Jesus claimed to be God that we have not touched on, including the claims he made at his trial. "It is sometimes argued that our Lord Himself never claimed to be divine. No doubt He had reasons for not doing so too openly, but He certainly did so repeatedly by implication. The chief charge at His trial was that He made Himself the Son of God, and He did not deny it" (Mt 26:63, 64, and Jn. 19:7) (Hammond 1973, 95).

Another look at those verses makes Hammond's point. First, in Matthew, "But Jesus kept silent. And the high priest said to Him, 'I adjure You by the living God, that You tell us whether You are the Christ, the Son of God.'

Jesus said to him, "You have said it yourself; nevertheless I tell you, hereafter you will see THE SON OF MAN SITTING AT THE RIGHT HAND OF POWER, and COMING ON THE CLOUDS OF HEAVEN."

Then in John, "The Jews answered him, 'We have a law, and by that law He ought to die because He made Himself out to be the Son of God.'" Pilate then asks Jesus directly, and no denial is made. Berkouwer makes the same point from Matthew, but also adds an important note:

> The charge of blasphemy pursued Christ to the end and provided the decisive motivation for his ultimate condemnation. In the encounter between Christ and Caiaphas the high priest adjures him to tell the council whether he is the Christ, the Son of God. The answer is affirmative: "Thou has said," but he adds: "nevertheless I say unto you, Henceforth ye shall see the Son of man sitting at the right hand of Power, and coming on the clouds of heaven" (Matt. 26:64). This speech of exalted self-proclamation is qualified as evident blasphemy and becomes the immediate occasion of his final verdict. For having heard this speech, the high priest tore up his clothes and said: "He hath spoken blasphemy: what further need do we

have of witnesses? Behold, now ye have heard the blasphemy: what think ye? They answered and said, He is worthy of death." The charge pursues him even on the cross: "If thou art the Son of God, come down from the cross" (Matt. 27:40). "For he said, I am the Son of God" (Matt. 27:43) (Berkouwer 1955, 172-173).

American New Testament scholar Ben Witherington raises other interesting suggestions as to ways in which Jesus saw himself as God, as quoted by Lee Strobel:

"Look at his relationship with his disciples. Jesus had twelve disciples, yet notice that he's not one of the Twelve." While this may sound like a detail without a difference, Witherington said it's quite significant. "If the Twelve represent a renewed Israel, where does Jesus fit in?" he asked. "He's not just part of Israel, not merely part of the redeemed group, he's forming the group —just as God in the Old Testament formed his people and set up the twelve tribes of Israel. That's a clue about what Jesus thought of himself.

Witherington went on to describe a clue that can be found in Jesus's relationship with John the Baptist. "Jesus says, 'Of all people born of woman, John is the greatest man on earth.' Having said that, he even goes even further in his ministry than the Baptist did—by doing miracles, for example. What does that say about what he thinks of Himself? (Strobel 1998, 134).

Then, to make the point even stronger, Witherington goes on to make two more observations as to how Jesus saw himself:

"And his relationship with the religious leaders is perhaps the most revealing. Jesus makes the truly radical statement that it's not what enters a person that defiles him, but what comes out of his heart. Frankly, this sets aside huge portions of the Old Testament book of Leviticus, with its meticulous rules concerning purity.

"Now, the Pharisees didn't like this message. They wanted to keep things as they were, but Jesus said, 'No, God has further plans. He's doing a new thing.' We have to ask, What kind of person thinks he has the authority to set aside the divinely inspired Jewish Scriptures and supplant them with his own teaching?

"And what about his relationship—if we can call it that—with the Roman authorities? We have to ask why they crucified him. If he had merely been an innocuous sage telling nice little parables, how did he end up on a cross, especially at a Passover season, when no Jew wants any Jew to be executed? There had to be a reason why the sign over his head said, 'This is the King of the Jews.'"

Witherington let the last comment hang in the air, before providing the explanation himself: "Either Jesus had made that verbal claim," he said, "or someone clearly thought he did" (Strobel 1998, 134-135).

Now the question comes up after looking at all of this evidence: "So what?" I met the well-known motivational speaker "Tremendous" Jones a number of years ago. Mr. Jones was an insurance salesman and I remember him saying that when you sell insurance, and when you try to lead people to faith, it does not matter what else happens if you do not ask the person to sign on the dotted line. We want to move toward the dotted line in this chapter by asking why God became man and why you should sign on the dotted line and make a commitment of faith. St. Anselm is famous for asking the question *Cur Deus Homo?* Or *Why the God-Man?* We do not want to get as deep as Anselm did, but it is important to realize that it is the claim of the historic Christian faith, and I believe it is the claim of the Bible, that Jesus is fully God and fully human, both at the same time. Now certainly a bit of a mystery surrounds this idea, as we try to comprehend just how the two natures can function together. Understanding the two natures of Christ is very similar to trying to understand the Trinity. We want to look at just why all of this is important—what did it accomplish, and what difference does it make to us? If Christians are asking you to follow Jesus, just what are you getting into? And why is it so important that Jesus is fully God and fully human?

The central Christian claim is that coming to know God and finding salvation is what the faith is all about. If this is not possible unless Jesus if fully God and fully human, just how does all of this fit together?

Well let's start at the beginning. In the first few chapters of Genesis, we are told about the creation of human beings and their place in the world. They had a fellowship with God and they knew God as their Creator. God also gave them an understanding of what it meant to obey him and to recognize his position as Creator. God did this by placing before them one small command, that they might honor him. We are also told that these first humans chose to disobey God, which brought about a change in their lives and in creation. The result was that evil entered into the world. They lost their connection to God, as the fellowship was broken. Then, right from the beginning, God promised a restoration. In Genesis 3:14-15, God spoke to the serpent but, in doing so, also made a promise to the woman:

> The LORD God said to the serpent, 'Because you
> have done this, Cursed are you more than all cattle,

> And more than every beast of the field; On your
> belly you will go, And dust you will eat All the
> days of your life; And I will put enmity Between
> you and the woman, And between your seed and
> her seed; He shall bruise you on the head, And you
> shall bruise him on the heel.'

A human had turned from God. Would it not be fitting, would it not be just, that a human would pay the penalty? The promise here in Genesis is that a descendent of Eve, a human, would defeat the evil the serpent had brought into the world. But we also see that by the promise (covenant) of God, a human would pay the cost even as he defeats the evil one.

So the Messiah, the Savior, needs to be human. The humanity of Jesus means, for one thing, that Jesus understands us. The work of the Messiah included suffering in body and soul; the Messiah had to be human so that, in his suffering, he might understand our suffering. The suffering of the Messiah was prophesied by the prophets. Isaiah's fourth servant song starting in Isaiah 52 gives us a clear example. Isaiah spoke to Israel about the suffering servant, the Messiah, as if he had already come, making the claim that ...

> He was despised and forsaken of men,
> A man of sorrows, and acquainted with grief; ...
> Surely, our griefs He Himself bore,
> And our sorrows He carried; ...
> But he was pierced through for our transgressions,
> He was crushed for our iniquities."

In Acts 3:18, Peter said that all the prophecies were fulfilled in Jesus. "But the things which God announced beforehand by the mouth of all the prophets, that His Christ would suffer, He has thus fulfilled." The Old Testament sacrifices that had gone on for generations were a type, an image, of what the Messiah would do with his own life. The whole sacrificial system was fulfilled in Jesus, just as the author of Hebrews explains in Hebrews 9:11-15:

> But when Christ appeared as a high priest of the good things to come, He entered through the greater and more perfect tabernacle, not made with hands, that is to say, not of this creation; and not through the blood of goats and calves, but through His own blood, He entered the holy place once for all, having obtained eternal redemption. For if the blood of goats and bulls and the ashes of a heifer sprinkling those who have been defiled sanctify for the cleansing of the flesh, how much more will the blood of Christ, who through the eternal Spirit offered Himself without blemish to God, cleanse your conscience from dead works to serve the living God? For this reason He is the mediator of a new covenant, so that, since a death has taken place for the redemption of the transgressions that were committed under the first covenant, those who have been called may receive the promise of the eternal inheritance.

There needed to be a sinless human to make a sacrifice for others, because if Jesus had sinned, his life would be forfeit to death and punishment, just like all others. A sinful person could not atone for anyone else. The followers of Jesus, the ones who knew him best, claimed that he was this person. He was the one who could stand for others by his sinless human nature, as we have seen proclaimed in Hebrews 7:26: "For it is fitting that we should have such a high priest, holy, innocent, undefiled, separated from sinners and exalted above the heavens." This high priest Jesus, who can stand in our place because he is sinless, also can sympathize with us because he has experienced being human. "For we do not have a high priest who cannot sympathize with our weaknesses, but One who has been tempted in all things as we are, yet without sin. Therefore let us draw near with confidence to the throne of grace, so that we may receive mercy and find grace to help in time of need" (Hebrews 4:15-16).

The humanity of Jesus means that Jesus's death can actually apply to us. It counts for us because it was not some outsider, but rather was one of us, on the cross. Jesus was a priest who offered a sacrifice, a pure sacrifice, and the sacrifice was his own life—all in fulfillment of the promise God made in Genesis 3:15.

Our relationship with God can be restored because the division between humanity and God has been bridged. It had been broken by the disobedience of Adam, and now is restored by the obedient, perfect life of Jesus. We would add that the humanity of Jesus also means that Jesus becomes an example for us on our own walk of faith. We cannot be Jesus because there is more to him than just the human side. We can, however, see in his humanity and obedience an example to strive for. So we see all of this being accomplished by Jesus's humanity—but what about his deity?

That Jesus is God with us, God come to our world, tells us several things. First, it tells us that it is appropriate to worship Jesus and no one else. It also tells us that we may be reunited with God. Because Jesus is, in fact, God with us—and not merely an angel or another human—there is now a connection to God open to us. God has entered into our world, our space and time, to show us who God is and how we might come to know his presence.

Most importantly, Jesus's deity means that his sacrifice is big enough to apply to everyone. Being God, his sacrifice has infinite value. One human, even a perfect human, might offer their life for another—but the value of one life is only equal to the value of another, not all of humanity. Only God could make the sacrifice that could apply to all who come to believe in the work of that sacrifice by faith. Even the psalmist understood this, long before Jesus came to be with us:

No man can by any means redeem his brother
Or give to God a ransom for him—
For the redemption of his soul is costly,
And he should cease trying forever—
That he should live on eternally,
That he should not undergo decay.
For he sees that even wise men die;
The stupid and the senseless alike perish
And leave their wealth to others (Psalm 49:7-10).

Jesus's humanity made his suffering possible and his deity gave it infinite value. His humanity meant Jesus could suffer, and his deity meant he suffered for each of us individually and not just the whole human race. It would have been impossible for one who was only God to suffer, and equally impossible for one who was only human to overcome death through resurrection. This is why Christians have always emphasized the two natures of Christ: the weakness of his humanity suffered as a sacrifice for our sin and his deity overcame death through resurrection, so we, too, might be raised.

Have you ever noticed how often the temples of religions around the world include massive staircases, usually up to an altar, or the building itself is on a high place so you must walk up to the altar? This might merely represent the idea that their god or God is higher than us and should be lifted up and exalted. It might represent our thinking that we can make our way to God. The God of the Bible did not want steps at his altar (Exodus 20:22-26). The Biblical view is that we cannot work our way to God, because God comes to us. Paul understood this when he said, in Romans 5, that while we were helpless sinners, and even the enemies of God, Christ died for us.

God came to us. The second person of the Trinity took on humanity. He added it to his nature. Why did he do this? We have looked at a number of ways Jesus claimed to be God. His claim is important because, by taking on humanity, He revealed God to us. John 1:14 tells us, "And the Word became flesh, and dwelt among us, and we saw His glory, glory as of the only begotten from the Father, full of grace and truth." We see the glory of God in Jesus. He is the revelation of God to us and he is so in the ultimate sense. "No one has seen God at any time; the only begotten God who is in the bosom of the Father, He has explained Him" (John 1:18).

In John 14:7-9, Jesus told Philip that this role of revealer was central to Jesus. "'If you had known Me, you would have known My Father also; from now on you know Him, and have seen Him.' Philip said to Him, 'Lord, show us the Father, and it is enough for us.' Jesus said to him, 'Have I been so long with you, and yet you have not come to know Me, Philip? He who has seen Me has seen the Father; how can you say, 'Show us the Father'?"

Jesus also came into this world to save us, and to bring us back into a relationship with God. We have seen that claim already in John 3:17: "For God did not send the Son into the world to judge the world; but that the world should be saved through Him." This is the message the Apostles took from Jesus's claims. "It is a trustworthy statement, deserving full acceptance, that Christ Jesus came into the world to save sinners, among whom I am foremost of all. Yet for this reason I found mercy, so that in me as the foremost, Jesus Christ might demonstrate His perfect patience as an example for those who would believe in Him for eternal life" (1 Timothy 1:15-16).

The Apostles, with their Jewish heritage, saw in Jesus a fulfillment of the Law of God and a completion of its work. The whole sacrificial system of the Old Testament led up to the work of Jesus in coming to offer forgiveness to us by sacrificing himself. "For what the Law could not do, weak as it was through the flesh, God did: sending His own Son in the likeness of sinful flesh and as an offering for sin, He condemned sin in the flesh" (Romans 8:3). All of this was to bring us back to God and to adopt us into the family of God. Jesus came to reveal God, but also to unite us to God. "But when the fullness of time came, God sent forth His

Son, born of a woman, born under the Law, in order that He might redeem those who were under the Law, that we might receive the adoption as sons" (Galatians 4:4-5).

Jesus also came to free us from bondage. Evil in this world and in our lives can be a sneaky thing and an enslavement. It can fool us and dominate us. It can be like a camper I had when I was a camp counselor. This camper came back several years and could be great fun, but he had a talent for persuading all the other kids in the cabin to do things that got them into trouble. Meanwhile, he always remained on the sidelines, out of the trouble, just watching his handiwork. He could manipulate the best group into getting into trouble while avoiding it himself. We eventually figured this out and knew what to watch for when his name appeared on the roster.

We do not always think of it in these terms, but sin is a slavery. It binds us and controls us, and by our own will, we let it. It is now our nature to do evil. Not that we are as evil as we could be, and not that there is not some good in us as we bear the image of God in this world. But we are all broken and trying to be our own God, on some level. Jesus came to set us free from this bondage. In Hebrews 2:9-18, we see the description of our state and what Jesus did for us so that he "might deliver those who, through fear of death, were subject to slavery all their lives" (Hebrews 2:15).

People do some remarkable things, and some burdensome things, because they think those things will get them to God, or what they think is God. Jesus's claim to be God means he has brought God to us. He lived with us to make our burdens light.

It is time to decide if we are willing to sign on to follow Jesus. Jesus is who he claimed to be. He revealed to us the very nature and attributes of God. Believing in him will change your life and bring you eternal life. This is not just doctrine—this is what will take you into eternity. People might like to say that Jesus did not claim to be God, but the evidence says otherwise. He is the One worth following. He is Emanuel, God with us.

APPENDIX:
THE IMPOSSIBILITY OF AN
INFINITE REGRESS

WHEN WE TALK about God having the power to exist as part of the very nature of God; or when we talk about God being a necessary Being; or when we claim the universe must have had a beginning, almost always someone raises the possibility of the universe having always existed. Why couldn't the universe have just been around forever? Why not an infinite series of finite events that led up to today?

I have found that when I say that there can be no such thing as an infinite causal regress, skeptics and even some Christians question the statement. Yet many scholars have tried to illustrate that point.

Let's start with a definition. When we talk about an infinite series of real events going backward in time forever, we would be talking about an *actual infinite*. This is a series with no beginning. It could not have a beginning if the series of events leading up to today is infinite. There is another kind of infinite series that I think some people confuse with the actual infinite. It is possible to conceive of a series that starts today and adds one thing to another, one cause to one effect, on to infinity. This series is called a *potential infinite* since it has a beginning and the potential to continue on to infinity. When people talk about the universe always existing, they are talking about an *actual infinite* series of finite events that had no beginning but brings us up to today.

It's also important to distinguish between a purely mathematical infinite series and a real infinite series. Infinity is a valuable mathematical concept and an interesting philosophical idea, and it has been since Aristotle. But numbers are not actual things. You can think of an infinity of numbers, but you can't have an infinity of any finite things. Therefore, infinity is valid mathematically—but you could not have an infinity of apples. As I heard comedian Steven Wright say, "You can't have everything. Where would you put it?" Mathematical points have no dimension and they take up no space, so there can be an infinite number of mathematical points between me and my office door. There cannot, however, be an infinite number of real points between me and the office door.

This is the real problem for Zeno's paradox. Zeno tried to show that Parmenides's teaching that motion is an illusion was correct. (I often wonder if Parmenides lips moved when he taught this.) Zeno said that, to get to the door, I would first have to get half way, and then to get to the halfway point, I'd have to pass the halfway point between myself and the first halfway point ... and on to infinity. I could never get to the door. It might seem mathematically true that, since I have to pass an infinite number of points to get to my office door, I therefore can never get there: but I *do* get there. This is because there are not an infinite number of *real* points between me and the door, so I do actually cross them every time I need to get out of the office.

When we speak of a series of past events, we realize those events come to an end in the present. An infinite series cannot have an end, yet an infinite regress series ends today, because we have crossed all the points. In other words, if there is an infinite series of events leading up to today, we would have to pass over an infinite series of events to get to today—and that cannot happen. But here we are. Norman Geisler summarizes the point:

> There are two kinds of infinite series: mathematical
> and metaphysical (actual). Mathematical infinities

are abstract. The line between A and B can have an infinite number of points or dimensionless intersections of two lines. Actual infinities are concrete, and it is not possible to get an infinite number of actual entities between A and B no matter how small these entities may be. An actual infinite series (regress) is impossible. Since an infinite series has no beginning and since a series of moments succeed one another, no matter how long the series it would always be possible to add one more. But one more cannot be added to an infinite number. Hence, one can never reach an infinite number. One can only indefinitely add one more. Infinity can never be achieved. Second, an infinite number of moments can never be traversed. But the number of moments before today has been traversed. Otherwise today would never have come. Hence, there is not an infinite number of moments before today. Time began (Geisler, 1999, 366).

In discussions, it has always helped to point out that an infinite regress is impossible because we could never have reached today if there is an infinite series behind us. It also helps to note that an actual infinity cannot be reached. If you add one event to another, you never reach the end, because you can always add one more. If someone were to try to count to infinity, they would never get there. There is always one more number.

Now, one can almost sense the pressure mounting. "But you took a whole chapter to talk about God being infinite, and now you are saying that an actual infinity does not exist." No, what is being claimed is that an infinite series does not exist. God is not a series. An infinite series of things or events cannot exist, but God is not a thing or an event. Our very point is that God *IS*. God is not a series.

All of God is eternally present. God's nature is to exist, complete and infinite. What we are getting at is that you cannot build an infinite. There can only be an in infinite.

Let us try a few more examples and explanations. To claim an infinite regress is to claim an infinitely long series of falling dominos with no first domino pushed over. Since I teach logic, I tend to think in terms of a premise and a conclusion. If you have a series of premises, each of which depends on the previous premise, at least one of them must have some truth value. If each one depends on the previous one and none have truth value, then you will have no conclusion, for there is no truth in the whole system.

Think of the old telephone game, where one person whispers to the next person, on down the line until you see what the message sounds like at the end. If the person at the end has received no communication, and the one before her has received no communication, and on and on—then, if no individual has some communication to share, then there is no communication at all, even if an infinity of people are lined up. If my existence depends on what has come before me and that existence depends on what came before, and on and on, then, if no one has the power of existing, there would be no existence. We might be able to explain each particular thing or event by the one preceding it, but if that chain goes on forever, the chain itself has no explanation, no sufficient reason for being. R. C. Sproul shares how Frederick Copleston makes our point:

> My point is that what we call the world is intrinsically
> unintelligible, apart from the existence of God. You
> see, I don't believe that the infinity of the series of
> events—I mean a horizontal series, so to speak—if
> such an infinity could be proved, would be in the
> slightest degree relevant to the situation. If you
> add up chocolates you get chocolates after all and

not sheep. If you add up chocolates to infinity, you presumably get an infinite number of chocolates. So if you add up contingent beings to infinity, you still get contingent beings, not a necessary being. An infinite series of contingent beings will be, to my way of thinking, as unable to cause itself as one contingent being (Sproul, 1984, 119).

Along with this, we might note that all finite things come into and go out of existence. This is the nature of being contingent, of not being self-existent. Everything that exists either exists on its own because it has the power to be, or does not exist on its own and depends on something outside of itself for its existence. If it has the power to exist, then it must exist; it is a necessary being. If it is not a necessary being, then we must look for a sufficient cause for its existence.

The issue of time and the working out of all possible outcomes over and infinite span of time comes into play here. If the universe is a series of finite events and objects, then the whole series might or might not exist. That is, the possibility of not existing is real. If there have been an infinite number of events, over an infinite amount of time, before today, then by now, the one possibility of not existing would have happened, and existence would have ended.

As the idea of an infinite regress seeks to avoid the need for a first cause, not only does it fail, but the real issue is exposed. Why would the series exist at all? Why is there something rather than nothing? There are some—like Copleston, Aquinas, and mathematician David Hilbert—who would hold that an infinite causal regress is possible. But their claim is that this is only possible if there is a higher cause for the series. The series does not explain itself. If a room full of students in a classroom need a book and no one in the classroom has the book, then no one can borrow it and no one will get it, even if there are an infinite number of students. If nothing that exists has the power to exist on its own, then how could the series exist?

Since we mentioned David Hilbert, let's look at his famous hotel illustration as described by William Lane Craig:

> Let us imagine a hotel with a finite number of rooms. Suppose, furthermore, that all the rooms are full. When a new guest arrives asking for a room, the proprietor apologizes, "Sorry, all the rooms are full." But now let us image a hotel with an infinite number of rooms and suppose once more that all the rooms are full. There is not a single vacant room throughout the entire infinite hotel. Now suppose a new guest shows up, asking for a room. "But of course!" says the proprietor, and he immediately shifts the person in room #1 into room #2, the person in room #2 into room #3, the person in room #3 into room #4, and so on, out to infinity. As a result of these room changes, room #1 now becomes vacant and the new guest gratefully moves in. But remember, before he arrived all the rooms were full! Equally curious, according to the mathematicians, there are now no more persons in the hotel than there were before: the number is just infinite. But how can this be? (Craig, 1984, 76-77).

As we can see, the idea of an infinite regress leads us into all sorts of absurdities: conclusions that just do not work in reality. For instance, in the real world, if you have a series or number of things and you take some away, you are left with fewer than you started with. But not in an infinite series.

> ... an actual infinite series of past events is logically impossible. As we will see, this idea is simply incoherent. Let's begin by saying that time is the

succession of events. Without any "happenings," time does not exist. Time depends on events—whether physical or mental—for its existence. So we ask, "Could past time be infinite? Could the series of past events be beginningless?" If we subtract a number from an infinite series [1, 2, 3, ...} so that we then have {2, 3, 4, ...}, we still have the same amount of events (viz. an infinite number). This becomes a problem if we apply it to the world in which we live. Or what if we removed all odd numbers from an infinite series so that we had {2, 4, 6, ...}? Would this new set be any smaller than the set of all natural numbers {1, 2, 3, ...}? No. Strangely, both would be equal, mathematically speaking, but this is absurd when we talk about the everyday world. Furthermore, if the past is infinite and we assign to each past event a negative natural number{... -3, -2, -1, 0}, with 0 representing the present, then all of the negative numbers would have been enumerated, which is absurd. We can always add one more event yet still have the same outcome. Let's again assign to every event in the past a series of corresponding numbers {... -3, -2, -1}. If we assume that the series of past events is beginningless and therefore an infinite time had elapsed by the time of, say, Socrates, then would not *more than an infinite number* of events have been added by the present time? We would naturally think so, but an infinite number cannot be added to. At any point in the past, an infinite series of events has already elapsed. But how could this be since we have arrived at today? (Copan, 2001, 64-65).

While we are looking at negative numbers, let's look at another illustration used by Craig:

> Suppose we meet a man who claims to have been counting down from infinity and who is now finishing: …,-3, -2, -1, 0. We could ask, why didn't he finish counting yesterday. Or the day before or the year before? By then an infinite time had already elapsed, so that he should already have finished. Thus, at no point in the infinite past could we ever find the man finishing his countdown, for by that point he should already be done! In fact, no matter how far back into the past we go, we can never find the man counting at all, for at any point we reach, he will already have finished. But if at no point in the past do we find him counting, this contradicts the hypothesis that he has been counting from eternity (Craig, 2008, 124).

Maybe this math dealing with negative numbers is confusing, but notice that it describes exactly what an infinite regress claims: that we can pass through an infinite past and arrive at today. Maybe a less abstract illustration will help:

> If the number of past events were infinite, that would lead to infinities of different sizes. For suppose Jupiter completes an orbit once every twelve years and Saturn once every thirty years and the sphere of the stars once every thirty-six thousand years. If the universe is eternal and these planets have been orbiting from eternity, then each of these bodies has completed an infinite number of orbits, and one will have completed twice as many or thousands of times as many orbits as another, which is absurd.

Finally, if we take the orbits completed by just one of these planets, we may ask, is the number of orbits it has completed odd or even? It would have to be one or the other, and yet it is absurd to say the infinite is odd or even (Craig, 2008, 96-97).

In an infinite regress, we end up with a universe that is like a chain where one link is hanging from the one before it and on and on—except there is no first link and the chain is hanging in mid-air. In fact, Jonathan Edwards used this very image back in the 1700s. The idea of a Creator was very important to Edwards, partly because he saw no other option to explain the existence of the universe. Without the presupposition of a Creator, he had no answer. The notion that the material universe might have always existed, and the correlative notion of an infinite regression of finite causes and effects, Edwards deemed absurd. In Miscellany 880, he argues that an infinite series of finite effects needs an explanation or a cause just as much as any finite part of the series. He also used the illustration of a chain suspended in air and notes that the bottom link might be held up by the link above it, and this second link might be held up by the one above it, and so on. But ultimately, there is no explanation as to why the whole chain does not fall to the ground if there is no outside force holding up the chain (Townsend 1955, 89). The existence of a universe having infinite duration is untenable in Edwards's view:

> That something has been from all eternity, implies that there has been a duration past, which is without any beginning, which is an infinite duration: which is perfectly inconceivable, and is attended with difficulties that seem contrary to reason. For we cannot conceive how an infinite duration can be made greater, any more than how a line of infinite length can be made longer. But yet we see that past duration is continually added to.

If there were a duration past without beginning a thousand years ago, then that past infinite duration has now a thousand years added to it: and if so, it is greater than it was before by a thousand years; because the whole is greater than the part. Now the past duration consists of two parts, viz. that which was before the last thousand years, and that which is since. Thus here are seeming contradictions involved in this supposition of an infinite duration past (Edwards 1974, 2:481).

It might be that Edwards is doing two things here. He might be building a basis for a cosmological argument for the existence of God, but I would suggest that the tone and the context of these two statements show Edwards to be, in a negative fashion, describing the absurdity of the idea of an infinite regression.

So the idea of an infinite regress leads us into nothing but absurdities: infinities twice the size of other infinities, infinite time which we have somehow traversed to get to today, or a causal chain with no original cause. Contingent beings, no matter how many, cannot cause themselves. There must be a necessary being. If an infinite causal regress is not possible, then we are left with the idea that the universe had a beginning, and then we are left with the idea of a first cause: a being independent of anything else for its existence. Jesus, as he claimed to be God, was claiming to be that first cause, the Creator written about in the book of Genesis, Yahweh, God of the Jews: sovereign, omniscient, holy, and loving.

WORKS CITED

Archer, Gleason. 1982 *Encyclopedia of Bible Difficulties*. Grand Rapids, Michigan: Zondervan.

Bavinck, Herman. 1985. *The Doctrine of God*. Grand Rapids: Baker Book House.

Berkhof, Louis. 1986. *Systematic Theology.* Grand Rapids: Wm. B. Eerdmans. (Orig. pub. 1939.)

Berkouwer, G.C. 1954. *The Person of Christ*. Grand Rapids, Michigan: Eerdmans.

Bloom, Allan. 1987. The Closing of the American Mind: How Higher Education Has Failed Democracy and Impoverished the Souls of Today's Students. New York: Simon & Schuster.

Boettner, Loraine. 1960. *Studies In Theology*. 5th ed. Grand Rapids, Michigan: Wm. B. Eerdmans. (Orig. pub. 1947.)

Card, Michael. 1989. "Jubilee." Track 3 on *The Beginning*. Sparrow.

Castle, Tony, ed. 1983. *The New Book of Christian Quotations*. New York: Crossroads.

Copan, Paul. 2001. *That's Just Your Interpretation*. Grand Rapids, Michigan: Baker Books.

Craig, William Lane. 1984. *Apologetics: An Introduction*. Chicago: Moody Press.

-----. 2008. *Reasonable Faith: Christian Truth and Apologetics*. 3rd ed. Wheaton, Illinois: Crossway.

D'Souza, Dinesh. 2007. *What's So Great About Christianity*. Washington D.C.: Regnery Publishing.

Edwards, Jonathan. 1957. *The Works of Jonathan Edwards*. Vols. 1-13. New Haven: Yale University Press.

-----. 1974. *The Works of Jonathan Edwards*. Vols. 1 and 2. Edinburgh: Banner of Truth Trust.

Erickson, Millard J. 1995. *Christian Theology*. Grand Rapids, Michigan: Baker Book House.

Field, Benjamin. 1976. *The Students Handbook of Christian Theology*. Freeport PA: The Fountain Press. (Orig. pub. 1952.)

Flew, Anthony. 1967. "Miracles." in *The Encyclopedia of Philosophy*, edited by Paul Edwards. Vol. 5. New York: Macmillan and the Free Press.

Gathercole, Simon. 2014. "What Did the First Christians Think About Jesus?" in *How God Became Jesus*, edited by Michael F. Bird. Grand Rapids, MI: Zondervan; quoted in McDowell, Josh and McDowell, Sean. 2017. *Evidence That Demands A Verdict: Life-Changing Truth For A Skeptical World.*, Nashville, Tenn: Thomas Nelson.

Geisler, Norman L. 1984. *Christian Apologetics*. Grand Rapids, Michigan: Baker Books. (6th Printing)

-----. 1999. *Baker Encyclopedia of Christian Apologetics*. Grand Rapids, Michigan: Baker Books.

-----, and Brooks, Ronald M. 2001. *When Skeptics Ask*. Grand Rapids, Michigan; Baker Books. (Orig. pub. 1996.)

Guiness, Os. 1994. *Fit Bodies Fat Minds: Why Evangelicals Don't Think and What to do About It*. Grand Rapids, Michigan: Baker Books.

Guthrie, Donald. 1976. *The Pastoral Epistles*. Tyndale New Testament Commentaries. Grand Rapids: Wm B. Eerdmans.

Hammond, T. C. 1973. *In Understanding Be Men: A Handbook of Christian Doctrine*. Edited by David F. Wright. 6th ed. Downers Grove, Illinois: Inter-Varsity Press.

Hodge, Charles. 1997. *Systematic Theology. Vols. 1 and 2*. Grand Rapids, Michigan: Eerdmans. (Orig. pub. 1871).

Hoekema, Anthony A. 1974. "The Attributes of God: The Communicable Attributes." in *Basic Christian Doctrines,* edited by Carl F.H. Henry, 28-34. Grand Rapids: Baker Book House.

Kreeft, Peter, and Tacelli, Ronald. 1994. *Handbook of Christian Apologetics*. Downers Grove, Illinois: Inter-Varsity Press.

Lewis, C.S. 1947. *Miracles*. New York: Macmillan Co.

-----. 1952. *Mere Christianity*. Macmillan Paperback Edition. New York: Macmillan Co. (14th printing).

-----. 1976. *The Last Battle*. New York: Collier Books. (15th printing).

Litton, Edward Arthur. 1960. *Introduction to Dogmatic Theology*. Edited by Philip E. Hughes. Greenwood SC: The Attic Press.

Machen, J. Gresham. 2016. *The Person of Jesus*. Philadelphia: Westminster Seminary Press..

McDowell, Josh and McDowell Sean.2017. *Evidence That Demands A Verdict: Life-Changing Truth for a Skeptical World*. Nashville: Thomas Nelson.

Piper, John. 1995. *Future Grace*. Sisters, Oregon: Multnomah.

Schaeffer, Francis A. 1968. *Escape From Reason*. Downers Grove Illinois: Inter-Varsity Press.

-----. 1972a. *He Is There and He Is Not Silent.,* Wheaton: Tyndale.

-----. 1972b. *No Little People*. Downers Grove, Illinois: Inter-Varsity Press.

Sproul, R. C., and Gerstner, John, and Lindsley, Arthur. 1984. *Classical Apologetics: A Rational Defense of the Christian Faith and a Critique of Presuppositional Apologetics*. Grand Rapids: Academic Books.

-----. 1988. *Who Is Jesus?* Wheaton Illinois: Tyndale House.

-----. 1998. *The Holiness of God*. Wheaton, Illinois: Tyndale House.

Strobel, Lee. 1998. *The Case For Christ*. Grand Rapids, Michigan: Zondervan.

Thayer, Joseph Henry. 1974. *Thayer's Greek-English Lexicon of the New Testament*. Grand Rapids; Zondervan. (15th Printing)

Thomas, Robert L. ed. 1981. *New American Standard Exhaustive Concordance of the Bible: Hebrew-Aramaic and Greek Dictionaries*. Nashville: Holman.

Tolkien, J.R.R. 1966. "On Fairy Stories." in *The Tolkien Reader*. New York: Ballantine Books.

-----. 1977. *The Silmarillion*. Boston: Houghton Mifflin.

Townsend, Harvey G. ed. 1955. *The Philosophy of Jonathan Edwards From His Private Notebooks*. University of Oregon Monographs: Studies in Philosophy. Eugene: University of Oregon.

Zacharias, Ravi. 1996. *Deliver Us From Evil*. Dallas: Word Publishing.

-----. 2000. *Jesus Among Other Gods: The Absolute Claims of the Christian Message*. Nashville: Word Publishing.